Succeeding with SPANISH GRAMMAR

by
María Suárez Lasierra

with collaborations from
Estefanía Férez Bernal

BARRON'S

Author: **María Suárez Lasierra**
Collaborator: **Estafanía Férez Bernal**
English translation: **Eric Bye**

All inquiries should be addressed to:
Barron's Educational Series, Inc.
250 Wireless Boulevard
Hauppauge, NY 11788
http://www.barronseduc.com

ISBN-13: 978-0-7641-3659-7 (book only)
ISBN-10: 0-7641-3659-3 (book only)
ISBN-13: 978-0-7641-9341-5 (book and CD package)
ISBN-10: 0-7641-9341-4 (book and CD package)
Library of Congress Control Number: 2006929366

Printed in Canada
9 8 7 6 5 4 3 2 1

Welcome to the World of Spanish Grammar!

Would you like to learn Spanish grammar quickly, enjoyably, and enthusi-astically? Would you like to understand the rules thoroughly and be able to apply them?

In this course you will learn the most important grammatical aspects of the language. You will work intensively with grammar using a modern, commu-nication-based method, and will learn how to apply it in lifelike situations. At the same time you will acquire a solid basic knowledge of communica-tion, vocabulary, and geography through a variety of exercises. Because of its flexible approach, *Succeeding with Spanish Grammar* is appropriate for both beginners and people who have had some prior exposure to the language. Answer keys and tips will help you to master Spanish grammar as an independent learner.

How is this Book Structured?

This book consists of 12 modules and 12 tests. Each module begins with an easy introduction to the various subjects. There are also clear explanations, and you have the opportunity to use what you have learned in numerous exercises. After every module you can take a test to see if you really have mastered the contents.

The course is complemented by an audio CD; it contains many of the exer-cises and provides thorough practice for your listening comprehension, pronunciation, and oral communication. The exercises are numbered sequentially so it's easier for you to find where you are at a glance. This will also help you in checking the answers that are located in the appendix of the book.

Graphic Symbols

The graphic symbols tell if you need a pencil, an extra piece of paper, or the audio CD (always optional) for any given exercise:

 This symbol shows you that the exercise is also on the audio CD. The track number tells you where to find the exercise on the CD.

 For an exercise with this symbol you need a pencil to write down or enter something.

 You also need a pencil for these exercises, this time to check something off or to connect items.

With this symbol you are invited to use an additional piece of paper to do the exercise.

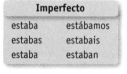 This symbol notifies you that you should pay particularly close attention to the material.

The box contains useful, interesting notes about the Spanish language and country-specific details.

mira – *look*
me llamo ... –
My name is...
¿quién eres? –
Who are you?

The vocabulary field contains words and expressions that are helpful in the exercises.

Imperfecto	
estaba	estábamos
estabas	estabais
estaba	estaban

This box contains verbs in their conjugated forms.

▶ § 5 Nouns

This grammar label tells you where you can find further information on a particular grammatical subject.

Appendix

Here you will find the following:

Answers: You can refer to the appendix to check your answers.

Grammar: Here you will find thorough explanations of all the important grammar contained in this course.

Glossary: In this alphabetical glossary you can quickly find all the words used in this book, along with their translations.

Have fun, and good luck in learning Spanish!

Table of Contents

Contents

1 TR.01

Read the minidialogue about saying hello and good-bye. You can also listen to the dialogue on the CD.

> **Valentina:** Hola, ¿qué tal? **Luis:** Muy bien, gracias.
> **Valentina:** Buenos días, me llamo Valentina, ¿y tú? **Alicia:** Soy Alicia. **Luis:** Buenas tardes, soy Luis. **Ángel:** Y yo soy Ángel.
> **Ángel:** Buenas noches. **José:** Adiós. **José:** Hasta pronto.
> **Ángel:** Hasta luego.

hola – *hello*
¿qué tal? –
How's it going?
me llamo... –
My name is...
yo soy... –
I am...
adiós – *Good-bye,*
so long
hasta pronto –
See you soon
hasta luego –
See you later

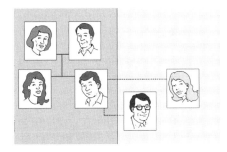

2 TR.02

Valentina introduces her family to you. Read the sentences. You can also listen to the sentences on the CD.

Hola, buenos días, soy Valentina.
Él es Luis. Es mi hermano.
Ésta es Carmen. Ella es mi madre.
Éste es mi padre, Ángel.
Alicia es la novia de Luis.
Éste es un amigo de Luis. Él es José.

él es... – *he is ...*
mi – *my*
el hermano –
the brother
la madre –
the mother
el padre – *the father*

*Introducing Oneself—the Verb **ser***

3

¡Bueno saber!

Buenos días is used in greeting people until around 1:00 P.M. Around the midday meal, approximately 2:00-3:00 P.M., people switch to **buenas tardes**. They say **buenas noches** starting at 8:00 or 9:00 P.M.; it means either *good evening* or *good night*.

▶ § 14 The Present Tense of **ser**

Several people introduce themselves in the following dialogue. Put the words into the appropriate spaces. You can also listen to the dialogue on the CD.

tardes – luego – yo – tal – tú – soy – adiós – llamo – gracias – es

Valentina: Buenas (1) _____.

Alicia: Hola, (2) _____ Alicia. Soy la novia de Luis.

Valentina: ¡Ah! Hola, encantada. (3) _____ soy Valentina. Soy la hermana de Luis.

Alicia: Es un placer.

Valentina: Pasa, por favor.
...

Alicia: Hola Luis. ¿Qué (4) _____?

Luis: Hola Alicia. Muy bien ¿y (5) _____?

Alicia: Muy bien también.

Luis: Mira, éste (6) _____ mi padre y ésta es mi madre.

Ángel: Hola Alicia, encantado. Yo soy el padre de Luis.

Carmen: Buenas tardes, Alicia. Me (7) _____ Carmen y soy la madre de Luis. ¿Quieres un café?

Alicia: Sí, muchas (8) _____.
...

Alicia: Muchas gracias por todo, (9) _____.

Luis: Hasta pronto, Alicia.

Ángel: Hasta (10) _____.

¡Bueno saber!

The familiar form of address is quite common in Spanish-speaking countries. It is used with old and young, particularly among family and friends.

4 TR.04

Spanish Pronunciation: Read the rules and try to pronounce the examples in parentheses. You can also listen to the examples on the CD.

1. **c** before **e**, **i**: soft like **s** sound; in Spain it is lisped; otherwise, hard like **k** (cacao, Cuba)
2. **ch** as in *child* (Chile, chico)
3. **g** before **e**, **i**: breathy, guttural sound like the initial sound of *chutzpah*; otherwise, like a hard **g** (Goya, Granada)
4. **h** is silent (hotel)
5. **j** like the **ch** in *chutzpah* (San José)
6. **ll** like initial sound of *yellow* (Mallorca, Sevilla)
7. **ñ** like the middle vowel sound in *cognac* (España)
8. **qu** like the sound of *coo*
9. **r** trilled; **rr** forcefully trilled (Roma, Andorra)
10. **z** like **s** (Zaragoza); in Spain it is lisped

5

Stress: Read the rules and try to pronounce the examples.

1. Words that end in a vowel, **-n**, or **-s** generally are stressed on the next-to-the-last syllable: **Cuba**, **Sevilla**.

2. Words that end with a consonant (except for **-n** and **-s**) generally are stressed on the last syllable: **hotel**, **hospital**.

3. All words that deviate from these rules carry an accent on the vowel in the stressed syllable: **café**, **túnel**.

4. Words that are stressed on the third syllable from the last always have an accent: **teléfono**, **América**.

6 👓

Perhaps you have already noticed that there are masculine and feminine nouns in Spanish. There is consequently a masculine and a feminine article:

▶ § 5 Nouns

	Singular	Plural
masculine	**el** herman**o**	**los** herman**os**
feminine	**la** herman**a**	**las** herman**as**

Nouns that end in **-o** generally are masculine; nouns that end in **-a** are feminine.

7 ✏

Now it's your turn! Write the articles in the following sentences:

    1. Luis es _____ hermano de Valentina.

    2. _____ novia de Luis se llama Alicia.

    3. Soy José, _____ amigo de Luis.

Nouns that end in **-e** or a consonant may be either masculine or feminine: **el padre**, **la madre**, etc.

There are a few exceptions, however: **la radio**, **la foto**, **el día**, **el clima**, etc.

8 ✏️

Write in the masculine (**el**) or feminine (**la**) articles.

1. _____ madre
2. _____ hermana
3. _____ niño
4. _____ niña
5. _____ amigo
6. _____ hermano
7. _____ hotel
8. _____ chico
9. _____ amiga
10. _____ padre
11. _____ novia
12. _____ foto

Learning Tip!

Always learn nouns in combination with their article. In Spanish it is very important to match adjectives with the gender and number of the nouns.

9 👓

The demonstrative pronouns **éste** and **ésta** are used for things or people that are right there with the speaker, especially in making introductions.

	Singular	
masculine	**este**	Éste es mi hermano, Luis.
feminine	**esta**	Ésta es mi novia, Alicia.

If **éste** or **ésta** is used to modify a noun, there is no written accent. If they replace a noun, they may have an accent.

Este hotel es muy bonito.   *This hotel is very nice.*
Éste es muy bonito.   *This one is very nice.*

¡Bueno saber!

The demonstrative pronoun **esto** can never be used in combination with a noun; it refers to a condition or a thing that is not mentioned specifically.
¿Qué es esto? – *What is this?*
Esto es todo. – *That's all.*

10 ✏

Match the demonstrative pronouns with the sentences.

> a. ésta   b. éste   c. éste   d. ésta

1. Hola, buenos días. _____ es mi padre.

   Se llama Ángel.

2. Y _____ es mi hermano.

3. Y _____ es mi madre.

4. José, _____ es mi amiga, María.

¡Bueno saber!

Usted (*you*, formal) is used with people you don't know well, or to whom you must show respect; **ustedes** (*you*, plural) is used in addressing several people. They are often abbreviated **Ud./Vd.** or **Uds./Vds.**

11 👓

	ser *(to be)* irregular verb	
yo	soy	*I am*
tú	eres	*you are*
él, ella, usted	es	*he is, she is, you (formal) are*
nosotros / as	somos	*we are*
vosotros / as	sois	*you (familiar pl.) are*
ellos / as, ustedes	son	*they are, you (pl.) are*

In Spanish, subject pronouns are rarely used; if they are, it's for differentiating among several people or for emphasis.

12 ✏

Match the subject pronouns with the sentences.

> ella – él – tú – ella – yo

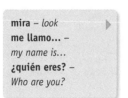

mira – *look*
me llamo... – *my name is...*
¿quién eres? – *Who are you?*

1. _____ soy José.

2. _____ es María.

3. Mira, _____ es José. Es un amigo de Barcelona.

4. _____ es Valentina. Es mi hermana. Es muy simpática.

5. Me llamo Carmen. Y _____, ¿quién eres?

13

Read the dialogues and decide which dialogue fits with which illustration.
You can also listen to the dialogues on the CD.

a. **Luis:** Alicia, te presento a un amigo. Se llama José.
Alicia: Encantada.
José: Encantado. ¿Qué tal?
Alicia: Muy bien, gracias.

b. **Valentina:** Mira, Luis, ésta es Cecilia. Es mi amiga de México.
Luis: Hola Cecilia. Es un placer.
Cecilia: Encantada.

c. **Ángel:** Alicia, te presento a mi mujer, Carmen.
Alicia: Mucho gusto. Soy Alicia.
Carmen: Hola Alicia. Encantada.

> **¡Bueno saber!**
> You can also introduce someone by saying **te / le presento a...** *May I introduce... Pleased to meet you* is **mucho gusto**, **es un placer**, or **encantado/a**. A man always says **encantado**; a woman says **encantada**. The other expressions are used in the same form by both.

14

Read the expressions. Then try to divide them into two categories:
saludos/despedidas (s/d) (*greetings and good-byes*) or **presentaciones (p)** (*introductions*). You can also listen to the expressions on the CD.

1. Adiós. Adiós. ☐
2. Me llamo Juana y ella es Pilar. ☐
3. Buenas tardes, Carmen. ☐
4. Es un placer. Yo soy Pedro. ☐
5. Te presento a Cecilia. ☐
6. Hola, ¿qué tal? ☐

15

Write the appropriate forms of the verb **ser** in the blanks.

1. vosotros _____

2. ellos _____

3. tú _____

4. yo _____

5. usted _____

6. nosotros _____

16

Read the questions and match them with the answers. You can also listen to the questions on the CD.

1. Hola Alicia, te presento a mi madre Carmen.

2. Buenos días, yo soy Pablo, y usted, ¿cómo se llama?

3. Te presento a Maite. Ella es de Barcelona.

4. ¿Tú eres Jorge?

5. Hola, Buenos días. ¿Vosotras sois de Sevilla?

6. Te presento a Valentina. Ella es mi hermana.

a. No, no soy Jorge. Me llamo Alejandro.

b. Hola, ¿qué tal, Valentina?

c. Hola Carmen, encantada.

d. Yo me llamo José, mucho gusto.

e. Sí, somos de Sevilla. Nosotras somos Pilar y Ana.

f. Buenas tardes, Maite. Es un placer.

*The Verb **ser**—Greetings and Good-byes*

1

Which verb form matches which subject pronoun?
Choose the correct answer.

1. **nosotras**
   - a) son
   - b) somos
   - c) soy

2. **yo**
   - a) somos
   - b) sois
   - c) soy

3. **ustedes**
   - a) es
   - b) sois
   - c) son

4. **tú**
   - a) eres
   - b) es
   - c) son

5. **él**
   - a) son
   - b) somos
   - c) es

6. **vosotros**
   - a) sois
   - b) es
   - c) eres

2

Try to divide the expressions into these categories: **saludos/despedidas (s/d)** *(greetings/good-byes)* or **presentaciones (p)** *(introductions)*.

1. ¿Qué tal? – Muy bien gracias. ☐
2. Adiós. ☐
3. Yo me llamo Valentina. ☐
4. Ésta es mi novia. ☐
5. Buenos días. ☐
6. Te presento a José. ☐
7. Hola. ☐
8. Es un placer. ☐
9. Ella es de Sevilla. ☐
10. Mucho gusto. ☐

*Articles: the Verb **ser***

3 🖉

Write the missing articles in the blanks:

1. _____ madre
2. _____ amigo
3. _____ padre
4. _____ foto
5. _____ chica
6. _____ niño

4 🖉

Write the missing conjugated forms of the verb **ser** in the blanks.

1. Yo _____ Lucía.
2. ¿Quién _____ tú?
3. No, no _____ Juan, Juan _____ él.
4. ¿Vosotras _____ Alicia y Viviana?
5. Sí, ellas _____ Alicia y Viviana.
6. Nosotras _____ de Sevilla.
7. ¿Quién _____ ella?
8. Ella _____ Mercedes.
9. Nosotros vivimos en Valencia pero _____ de Barcelona.
10. Pilar y Juana _____ de Madrid.

1

Match the sentences with the appropriate pictures.

a. Miguel es de México.
b. Pablo es de Cuba.
c. Mariela y Josefa son de Perú.
d. Juana es de Sevilla.
e. Fabiola y Martín son de Buenos Aires.

2

Read the forms of the regular **-ar** verb **trabajar** (*to work*), and try to pronounce them. You can listen to the forms on the CD.

1. yo **trabajo**
2. tú **trabajas**
3. él, ella, usted **trabaja**
4. nosotros, nosotras **trabajamos**
5. vosotros, vosotras **trabajáis**
6. ellos, ellas, ustedes **trabajan**

2

Regular Verbs Ending in -ar, -er, -ir

§ 13 Regular Verbs

¡Bueno saber!

The question mark designates a question. It appears upside down at the beginning of a question.
¿...?
The exclamation point indicates an expression of enthusiasm or surprise, etc. It appears upside down at the beginning of an exclamation.
¡...!

no todos – *not all*
pero – *but*
la enfermera – *the nurse*
¿verdad? – *right?*
el / la médico / a – *the doctor*
el hospital – *the hospital*
el / la estudiante – *student*
Derecho – *law*

¡Bueno saber!

Some professional designations have a masculine and a feminine form; others have only one form for both sexes: **el maestro / la maestra, el / la cantante.** You can use the following to ask a person about their profession: **¿Qué hace (usted)?** (respectful) *What do you do?* **¿Qué haces?** (informal) *What do you do?*

3

Read the dialogue between Valentina's family and Alicia, Luis's friend. You can also listen to the dialogue on the CD.

Carmen:	Alicia, ¿de dónde eres?
Alicia:	Soy de Madrid. Y ustedes, ¿son de Zaragoza?
Carmen:	No todos. Valentina y Luis sí son de Zaragoza, pero Ángel es de Huesca y yo soy de Madrid.
Ángel:	¿Y tú familia, de dónde es?
Alicia:	También es de Madrid.
Valentina:	Tú eres enfermera, ¿verdad?
Alicia:	No, no soy enfermera. Soy médica.
Valentina:	¿Dónde trabajas?
Alicia:	Trabajo en un hospital en Madrid. ¿Y tú?
Valentina:	Yo soy estudiante de Derecho.
Carmen:	¿Quién quiere café?

Can you deduce from the text how to say from where in Spanish?

from where? – _____

4

You are already familiar with regular **-ar** verbs. Now come the regular **-er** and **-ir** verbs.

Verb forms consist of a word stem and an ending. Depending on their ending (**-ar**, **-er**, or **-ir**), Spanish verbs are divided into three conjugations: trabaj-**ar**, beb-**er**, viv-**ir**.

Instead of using the infinitive endings, the appropriate endings for the various persons are added.

	trabajar	beber	vivir
yo	trabaj**o**	beb**o**	viv**o**
tú	trabaj**as**	beb**es**	viv**es**
él, ella, usted	trabaj**a**	beb**e**	viv**e**
nosotros, nosotras	trabaj**amos**	beb**emos**	viv**imos**
vosotros, vosotras	trabaj**áis**	beb**éis**	viv**ís**
ellos, ellas, ustedes	trabaj**an**	beb**en**	viv**en**

5

Complete the sentences by choosing the correct verb forms.

1. Alicia *trabajan / trabaja / trabajamos* en un hospital.

2. Los españoles *comen / coméis / come* paella.

3. La familia de Valentina *viven / vivimos / vive* en España.

4. Yo *trabajo / trabajáis / trabajamos* en un hotel.

6

Here are the indefinite articles in Spanish:

	Singular	Plural
masculine	**uno**	**unos**
feminine	**una**	**unas**

They agree in gender and number with the nouns they accompany. Usually no indefinite article is used in the plural. The plural form serves as an indefinite expression of quantity.

Compro unos tomates.   *I buy a few tomatoes.*

7

Put the indefinite articles into the appropriate spaces.

> un – una – unos – unas

1. Juan y Pedro son _____ amigos de Alicia.

2. En Barcelona hay _____ casas muy bonitas.

3. En la ciudad hay _____ iglesia muy bonita.

4. Soy médica y trabajo en _____ hospital.

el hospital –
the hospital
la ciudad – *the city*
la casa – *the house*
bonito/a –
handsome, pretty

The Indefinite Article—Plural Formation

8

Read the terms and try to pronounce them. You can also listen to the words on the CD.

el libro – *the book* ▶
la silla – *the chair*
la mesa – *the table*
el teléfono – *the telephone*
el ordenador (Spain) – *the computer*
el fax – *the fax*
la lámpara – *the lamp*
el móvil (Spain) – *the cell phone*
el bolígrafo – *the ballpoint pen*
el cuaderno – *the notebook*
Note: In Latin America, **el ordenador** becomes **la computadora**, and **el móvil** becomes **el celular.**

un libro, unos libros

una silla, unas sillas

una mesa, unas mesas

un teléfono, unos teléfonos

un ordenador, unos ordenadores

un fax, unos faxes

una lámpara, unas lámparas

un móvil, unos móviles

un bolígrafo, unos bolígrafos

un cuaderno, unos cuadernos

9

You have become familiar with the singular and plural of various objects. Can you now figure out the rule for plural formation?

To make the plural of words that end in a vowel, we add an _____.

To words that end with a consonant, we add _____.

10 👓

Negation in Spanish:
No can mean both *no* and *not*. It is always placed before the verb.

Yo **no** soy Valentina, soy Alicia. *(I am not Valentina; I am Alicia.)*
No, **no** como carne. *(No, I don't eat meat.)*

11 📼 ✏️

Try to negate the examples provided. You can also listen to the answers.

1. Yo soy Valentina. _____, soy Alicia.

2. Somos de Chile. _____, somos argentinos.

3. Trabajo en un hospital. _____, trabajo en una peluquería.

4. Como carne. No, _____. Sólo como verdura, fruta, etc.

> **¡Bueno saber!**
> Note the differences in the following sentences: **No soy de Lima.** (*I am not from Lima.*) **No, soy de Lima.** (*No, I am from Lima.*) In the second sentence there is a brief pause after **no**, so the difference is clear. Double negatives are also possible. **No, no soy de Lima.** (*No, I am not from Lima.*)

12 👓

You can use the following expressions to ask where a person is from or to answer that type of question:

¿De dónde eres? *(Where are you from?)*
Soy de Ecuador. ¿Y tú? *(I'm from Ecuador. How about you?)*
¿De dónde es (usted)? *(Where are you from?)*
(Yo) soy de Paraguay. *(I am from Paraguay.)*

If you already have an idea you can use the following expressions:

¿Eres de Caracas? *(Are you from Caracas?)*
Sí, soy de Caracas. *(Yes, I am from Caracas.)*
¿Es (usted) de Guatemala? *(Are you from Guatemala?)*
No soy de Guatemala. Soy de Perú. *(I am not from Guatemala. I am from Perú.)*

13 ✎

Now it's your turn! Match the words with the appropriate blanks.

> soy – de – dónde – eres

1. ¿De _____ es usted, señor Domínguez?

2. Yo soy _____ la capital de Ecuador, de Quito.

3. Miguel, ¿_____ de México?

4. No _____ de México, soy de Cuba.

14 ✎

Put the correct verb forms into the blanks.

¡Bueno saber!

The same endings are used for all regular verbs in a group. Note the accent in the second person plural: **habláis, bebéis, vivís.**

comer – *to eat* ▶
tomar –
to take, to drink
vivir – *to live*
estudiar – *to study*
trabajar – *to work*
viajar – *to travel*
comprender –
to understand

1. Los amigos de Valentina _____ en Madrid.

2. Valentina _____ en la Universidad

   Complutense de Madrid.

3. No _____ esta palabra.

4. ¿Pablo y tú _____ en un hospital?

5. ¿Vosotras _____ un café?

6. ¿Tú _____ mucho a España?

7. Nosotros _____ en un restaurante.

8. Yo soy actor y _____ en un teatro.

> a. comemos   b. tomáis   c. viven   d. estudia
>
> e. trabajo   f. viajas   g. comprendo   h. trabajáis

15 ✏️

You have already become familiar with the indefinite article. Look at the pictures and write the correct indefinite article in the blanks.

1. En esta foto vemos _____ amigos de Valentina y Luis.

2. En el salón hay _____ mesa antigua.

3. Quiero comprar _____ sillas modernas de metal.

4. Luis lee _____ libro interesante.

16 ✏️

Mark off the term that is in the plural.

1. país – ciudad – ciudades – pueblo
2. un – una – uno – unas
3. amigos – chico – camarero – señor
4. hermano – hermanas – hermanito – hermana
5. este – estos – esta – esto
6. televisión – teléfonos – ordenador – libro

17 ✏

Look at the pictures and write the appropriate term in the blank, along with the indefinite article. Note whether you see one or more objects. Watch out for the accents.

——————————— ——————————— ———————————

——————————— ——————————— ——————————— ———————————

——————————— ——————————— ———————————

Questions and Answers—Regular Verbs

1

Answer the question and choose the appropriate answer. There is only one correct answer.

1. ¿De dónde eres?

   ▪ a. Sí, vivimos en Madrid.
   ▪ b. Soy de Zaragoza.
   ▪ c. No, no trabajo en
      un hospital.

2. ¿Son de Venezuela?

   ▪ a. No, somos de Bolivia.
   ▪ b. Sí, yo soy de Bilbao.
   ▪ c. No, María toma
      un café.

3. ¿Vive usted en Buenos Aires?

   ▪ a. No, trabajamos en una
      farmacia.
   ▪ b. Sí, ellos viven en
      Montevideo.
   ▪ c. Sí, yo vivo allí.

4. ¿Son ustedes de Bilbao?

   ▪ a. No, somos de Vigo.

   ▪ b. No somos de Vigo.
   ▪ c. Sí, somos de Granada.

2

Read the sentences. Which verb form is correct? Choose the correct term.

1. ¿María y tú *vivís / vive / vivo* en Madrid?

2. Nosotros *trabajan / trabajáis / trabajamos* en una farmacia.

3. Ellos *tomo / toman / toma* café en el restaurante.

4. ¿Tú *comprendéis / comprenden / comprendes* todo?

5. Yo *trabajo / trabaja / trabajas* en la Escuela Oficial de Idiomas.

6. Miguel *escribo / escribís / escribe* una postal.

Plural

3 🖉

Look at the pictures and write the appropriate term in the blanks.
Pay attention to singular and plural, as well as the accents.

_____ _____ _____

_____ _____ _____

1 TR. 12

Read the sentences and try to pronounce them.
You can also listen to the sentences on the CD.

1. ¿Qué tal?
   Estoy muy bien.

2. ¿Cómo está José?
   José está enfermo.

3. ¿Cómo estáis?
   Estamos cansadas.

4. Valentina está
   triste.

5. Están en el jardín.

6. Están muy
   enamorados.

7. Cecilia está
   muy alegre.

8. ¿Dónde estás?
   Estoy en Barcelona.

9. ¿Cómo estás?
   Estoy nervioso.

2 🖊

▶ § 6 Adjectives

Match the pictures with the appropriate words.

¡Bueno saber!

Adjectives always agree in gender and number with the nouns they modify. This applies even when the adjective comes before the verb.

En esta ciudad hay casas modernas.

En esta ciudad hay muchas casas modernas.

1. ☐

2. ☐

3. ☐

a. las rosas rojas
b. la chica guapa
c. el libro amarillo
d. las casas modernas
e. los coches rápidos

4. ☐

5. ☐

3 💿 TR. 13 👓

Read the dialogue and try to pronounce the sentences correctly.
You can listen to the dialogue on the CD.

enfermo/a – *sick*
un poco –
a little
resfriado/a – *sick
with a cold*
la cama – *the bed*
el líquido –
the liquid
mejorar –
to get better
recuerdos a... –
greetings to...
que se mejore –
get well

José:	Hola Valentina. ¿Qué tal estás?
Valentina:	Yo estoy muy bien, gracias.
José:	Ya veo, estás muy guapa. Y, ¿cómo está Luis?
Valentina:	Luis está enfermo.
José:	¡Sí! ¿Está muy enfermo?
Valentina:	No, está un poco resfriado.
José:	¿Dónde está?
Valentina:	Hoy no trabaja. Está en casa, en la cama.
José:	Cuando yo estoy resfriado bebo mucho líquido y mejoro rápidamente.
Valentina:	Luis trabaja demasiado. Vivir tranquilamente es la mejor medicina para no enfermar.
José:	Recuerdos a Luis y que se mejore.
Valentina:	Gracias y hasta pronto.
José:	Adiós, adiós...

4

Estar is an irregular verb. It is used in asking about or expressing a personal condition or geographic location, and temporary or changeable circumstances.

	estar
yo	estoy
tú	estás
él, ella, usted	está
nosotros / as	estamos
vosotros / as	estáis
ellos / as, ustedes	están

Insert the appropriate form of the verb **estar** into the following sentences. You can also listen to the sentences on the CD.

¡Bueno saber!
Question words such as **cómo** (*how*), **dónde** (*where*), **qué** (*what*), etc. always have an accent in Spanish.

1. ¿Cómo _____ usted?

   _____ bien, gracias.

2. ¿Dónde _____ ustedes?

   _____ en la calle Velázquez.

5

1. Adjectives always agree in gender and number with the nouns they modify: las chic**as** guap**as** (*the pretty girls*)
2. Adjectives that end in **-o** change to **-a** in the feminine form. (The same rules as with nouns apply to plural formation.):
   el libro roj**o** (*the red book*)   la falda roj**a** (*the red skirt*)
3. Adjectives that end in **-e** or a consonant have just one form for masculine and feminine. (The same rules as with nouns apply to plural formation.):
   la cas**a** grand**e** / las cas**as** grand**es** (*the big house / the big houses*)
   el coch**e** grand**e** / los coch**es** grand**es** (*the big car / the big cars*)
   Generally the adjective comes after the noun in Spanish.

¡Bueno saber!
Mucho and **poco** function as adjectives when accompanied by a noun. Then they generally come before the noun. They too agree in gender and number with the noun: **Muchas ciudades son grandes.** (*Many cities are large.*)

6

Match up the appropriate words with the sentences.

la ciudad – *the city*
fantástico/a –
wonderful
grande – *large*
el centro histórico –
the old city
bonito/a – *pretty*
simpático/a –
nice

1. Barcelona es una ciudad _____.
2. Estos son libros _____.
3. El centro _____ es bonito.
4. Cecilia y Valentina son chicas _____.

a. histórico   b. fantástica   c. simpáticas   d. interesantes

¡Bueno saber!

There are some other adjectives that can come before the nouns, for example, **bueno, malo, primero, tercero, uno, alguno, ninguno**, etc. Then they lose the final **-o** of the masculine singular form, for example, **un chico bueno, un buen chico.**

7

An adverb modifies a verb, an adjective, another adverb, or an entire sentence. Adverbs are invariable.

Muy (*very*) accompanies an adjective or an adverb. **Mucho** (*very, much*) and **poco** (*not much*) either stand alone or accompany a verb when they are used as adverbs. **Bien** and **mal** are adverbs; they mean *well* and *poorly*, respectively.

Estoy **muy** bien. (*I am very well.*)

Trabajo **mucho**. (*I work a lot.*)

8

Read the following sentences. Decide which of the pictured situations
is appropriate. You can also listen to the sentences on the CD.

1. Luis está muy enfermo. ☐   2. Valentina está muy guapa. ☐

3. Luis trabaja mucho. ☐   4. La mujer está muy bien ☐

5. Los niños comen poco. ☐   6. Las personas están mal. ☐

9

In Spanish, designations of nationality are always adjectives. They can be classified according to their endings. If an adjective of nationality ends in a consonant, the feminine form adds a final **-a**:

inglés / inglesa

Note: **belga, iraquí, israelí** plus adjectives of nationality that end in **-(i)ense**, have the same form for both masculine and feminine.

The verb **ser** + adjectives of nationality
Example: **Yo soy norteamericano.** (masculine singular) / **Yo soy norte-americana.** (feminine singular) / **Nosotros somos norteamericanos** (masculine plural) / **Nosotras somos norteamericanas** (feminine plural).

Adjectives of nationality agree in gender and number.

Now it's your turn! Match the adjectives of nationality with the following sentences. You can also listen to the sentences on the CD.

1. **Ana:**	Yo soy	■		a. españoles
2. **Juan:**	Yo soy	■		b. chilena
3. **Luis y Valentina:**	Nosotros somos	■		c. cubano

10

Choose the correct form of the adjective.

1. Mijas es un pueblo *pequeño / pequeña / pequeños*.

2. José tiene amigas *simpáticos / simpática / simpáticas*.

3. Las oficinas de la empresa son *modernos /moderna / modernas*.

4. Buenos Aires y Sao Paulo son ciudades *gran / grandes / grande*.

5. En Barcelona hay *pocos / poco / pocas* parques.

6. En Estados Unidos *muchas / mucha / muchos* gente habla español.

7. En Barcelona hay *muchas / muchos / mucha* actividades culturales.

8. La ciudad tiene edificios *antiguo / antiguas / antiguos*.

11

Write the missing adjectives of nationality in the spaces. Watch for correct gender and number!

> § 7 Adjectives of Nationality

1. El señor Dupont es de París. Él es _____.

2. La señora Pardo es _____. Es de Barcelona.

3. Los amigos de Valentina son de Roma. Ellos son _____.

4. Las amigas de Cecilia son _____, de Ciudad de México.

5. Elke Losch es de Hamburgo. Ella es _____.

6. Yo soy Louis Lacroix, de Bruselas. Soy _____.

7. Me llamo Marco Oliveira, soy de Lisboa. Soy _____.

8. Alexandra Stark y Susanne Mayer son de Basilea.

    Son _____.

> **Bruselas** – *Brussels*
> **Lisboa** – *Lisbon*
> **Basilea** – *Basel*
> **Hamburgo** – *Hamburg*

12

Match the questions with the appropriate answers.

la llave – *the key*
la puerta – *the door*
sano/a – *healthy*
enfrente de –
facing, across from
la computadora –
the computer

1. ¿Dónde está Madrid?

2. ¿Dónde están las llaves?

3. ¿Qué tal estás?

4. ¿Tus amigos están enfermos?

5. ¿Dónde estás ahora?

6. ¿Dónde están en Mallorca?

a. Estamos en un hotel precioso en Palma de Mallorca.

b. Las llaves están en la puerta.

c. Madrid está en España.

d. Ahora estoy enfrente de la computadora.

e. Estoy muy bien, gracias.

f. No, mis amigos están sanos.

13

What does your city or town look like? Mark a **T** or an **F** to indicate if the following statements apply to your city.

En mi ciudad hay mucho tráfico.

Hay muchas actividades culturales.

¿Monumentos grandes? Sí, hay muchos monumentos.

Hay pocas casas modernas.

Los edificios son bonitos y antiguos.

La gente es simpática y muy agradable.

En mi ciudad hay muchas zonas verdes.

Mi ciudad tiene muchos cines, teatros y museos.

ser and *estar*

1 ✎

Answer the questions and select the appropriate answer. There is just one correct answer.

1. ¿Dónde está Valentina?

   ▨ a. Valentina está en Madrid.
   ▨ b. Valentina está enferma.
   ▨ c. Valentina es guapa.

2. ¿Quién está enfermo?

   ▨ a. Luis está mal.
   ▨ b. José está muy bien.
   ▨ c. Valentina y Luis son hermanos.

3. ¿Estás en Mallorca en un hotel?

   ▨ a. Sí, el hotel es muy bonito.
   ▨ b. Seguramente el hotel está en Mallorca.
   ▨ c. No, estoy en Madrid en mi casa.

4. ¿Qué tal están?

   ▨ a. Sí, está muy mal.
   ▨ b. Estamos muy bien.
   ▨ c. Están bastante bien.

5. ¿Quién está en el hospital?

   ▨ a. Miguel está en el hospital.
   ▨ b. El hospital está en Marbella.
   ▨ c. No, no estoy en el hospital.

6. ¿Dónde está Andalucía?

   ▨ a. Andalucía es una región.
   ▨ b. Andalucía es muy interesante.
   ▨ c. Andalucía está en el sur de España.

2 ✎

Write the missing forms of **ser** or **estar** in the blanks.

1. Madrid _____ una ciudad bonita.

2. Luis _____ enfermo.

3. Valentina _____ una chica muy simpática.

4. El hotel _____ en Palma de Mallorca.

5. Cecilia _____ mexicana.

*Adjectives—**muy** and **mucho***

3

Which adjective is appropriate for each illustration? Choose the adjective that agrees in gender and number with the noun.

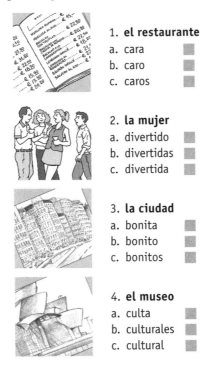

1. el restaurante
a. cara ▨
b. caro ▨
c. caros ▨

2. la mujer
a. divertido ▨
b. divertidas ▨
c. divertida ▨

3. la ciudad
a. bonita ▨
b. bonito ▨
c. bonitos ▨

4. el museo
a. culta ▨
b. culturales ▨
c. cultural ▨

4 🖉

Write the missing words in the spaces. Choose between **mucho** (*much, a lot*) and **muy** (*very*).

1. Valentina está _____ guapa.

2. Luis trabaja _____ en la oficina.

3. Los niños comen _____ chocolate.

4. Las personas viajan _____ en autobús.

5. Los padres de Valentina son _____ simpáticos.

6. Berlín está _____ lejos de Madrid.

7. Alicia trabaja _____ en el hospital.

8. España es un país _____ interesante.

ser and estar

1

Read the sentences about Ecuador and try to deduce the difference between **ser** and **estar**. You can also listen to the sentences on the CD.

§ 19 **ser / estar**

Ecuador **está** en el norte de Sudamérica.

Es un país muy interesante.

La capital de Ecuador **es** Quito.

El Chimborazo **es** un volcán con una altura de 6310 m.

Es un volcán activo.

La selva amazónica en Ecuador **es** muy grande y diversa.

Las Islas Galápagos **están** a unos 1000 km de Ecuador.

Las ciudades más bonitas **son** Cuenca y Quito.

La mayoría de los habitantes **son** indígenas.

La Panamericana **es** una carretera que atraviesa todo el país de norte a sur.

en el norte –
in the north
el país – *the country*
la capital – *the capital*
el volcán – *the volcano*
la altura – *the altitude*
la selva amazónica –
the Amazon jungle
la isla – *the island*
la mayoría –
the majority
los habitantes –
the inhabitants
la carretera –
the highway

*The Uses of **ser** and **estar***

2 👓

In Spanish there are two verbs for the verb *to be*: **ser** and **estar**.

Ser is used for such purposes as

• Identification:	Paula **es** mi hermana.
• Specifying origin, nationality, religion, and profession:	Paula **es** de Chile. / **es** chilena.
• Specifying permanent external and personality traits:	Paula **es** delgada. / **es** simpática.
• Definitions:	Santiago **es** la capital de Chile.
• Material, color:	El coche **es** azul.

Estar is used for such purposes as:

• Specifying geographical location:	**Estoy** en Valdivia.
• Describing how someone feels:	¿Cómo **estás**?
• Specifying temporary or changeable conditions:	Luis **está** enfermo.

3 ✏️

Ser or **estar**? Complete the sentences by writing the missing verbs in the blanks.

1. La catedral _____ en el centro de la ciudad.

2. Silvia _____ de Guadalajara pero vive en Madrid.

3. Yo _____ Ana. _____ española. Hoy _____ enferma.

4

Read the sentences about Valentina's vacation plans. She is talking about the future. Notice how that is expressed. You can also listen to the sentences on the CD.

▶ § 23 Infinitive
constructions:
ir a + infinitive

1. En verano **voy a viajar** a Ecuador.
2. Antes del viaje **voy a leer** una guía turística.
3. Quiero ver el Chimborazo por eso **voy a ir** a los Andes.
4. Y además **voy a nadar** en el Océano Pacífico.
5. **Voy a llevar** mi cámara fotográfica para hacer muchas fotos.
6. En Cuenca **voy a comprar** mucha artesanía porque me encanta.
7. Como hay muchos mosquitos **voy a llevar** un repelente.
8. También **voy a ver** las Islas Galápagos.

en verano –
in the summer
viajar – *to travel*
la guía turística –
the tour guide
por eso – *therefore*
nadar – *to swim*
el repelente –
the insect repellent

5

The verb **ir** is also used in combination with the preposition **a** to show direction or destination: **ir + a**

> **Voy a** América. *(I am going to America.)*

Careful: the verb **ir** *(to go)* is irregular:

yo	**voy**
tú	**vas**
él / ella / usted	**va**
nosotros / nosotras	**vamos**
vosotros / vosotras	**vais**
ellos / ellas / ustedes	**van**

¡Bueno saber!
The masculine singular definite article **el** combines with the prepositions **a** and **de**. The preposition
a + el = al
The preposition
de + el = del

Now it's your turn! Match up the following forms of the verb **ir** with the sentences.

> van – va – voy

1. Estoy enferma y _____ al médico.

2. Valentina _____ a Ecuador en las vacaciones.

3. Ellos _____ al supermercado.

4

Infinitive Constructions

6

¡Bueno saber!

In many regions this is the preferred future form, and the future construction is considered more formal.
Mañana va a ser la gran fiesta. (ir a + infinitive)
Mañana será la gran fiesta. (future)

ir a + infinitive is often used to designate the future, especially when the action is considered imminent, when an opinion is expressed, or when people speak about future plans.

> **Voy a viajar** a Ecuador de vacaciones.
> *(I'm going to travel to Ecuador for vacation.)*

Complete the following sentences by supplying the correct future expression.

1. El martes tú _____ ir al gimnasio.

2. El miércoles ella _____ ir al supermercado.

3. El viernes ustedes _____ ir al restaurante.

4. El fin de semana ellos _____ ir de excursión.

7

¡Bueno saber!

Expressions that are used to talk about the future:
vas a ir –
you are going to go
voy a ir – *I'm going to go*
voy a visitar –
I'm going to visit
voy a hacer –
I'm going to make / do

¡Bueno saber!

The question **¿a dónde...?** means *to where? It can also be written together as **¿adónde?**

Read the dialogue between Valentina and her friend Cecilia, a Mexican. Mark the expressions that deal with the future. You can also listen to the dialogue on the CD.

Cecilia: Hola Valentina, ¿a dónde vas a ir de vacaciones en septiembre?

Valentina: Todavía no estoy segura. Creo que voy a ir a Ecuador.

Cecilia: Ecuador es un país precioso. Hay muchos paisajes diferentes. Hay de todo: selva, montaña, mar... Además, es un mes fantástico para visitar las Islas Galápagos.

Valentina: ¿A cuántos kilómetros están las Islas Galápagos?

Cecilia: Están en el Pacífico, a unos 1000 kilómetros de la costa.

Valentina: Sí, voy a visitar las islas. ¿Cómo llego a las Galápagos?

Cecilia: Vas en avión desde Guayaquil. Y en las Galápagos visitas las islas en barco. Lleva una cámara fotográfica porque hay animales muy exóticos.

Valentina: Voy a hacer muchas fotos, no te preocupes. Y, en el interior del país ¿qué hay?

Cecilia: Pues, en el interior del país...

8

Hay and **está/n** are used with questions and statements about whether something exists or where something is located. When do you use **hay** and **está/n**?

Hay *(there is / are)*: the speaker is not referring to a specific thing. It is used with an indefinite article.

¿Hay un hotel bueno en Quito? *(Is there a good hotel in Quito?)*

Está/n: The speaker is referring to a specific thing. It is used with a definite article.

¿Dónde está el Gran Hotel en Quito? *(Where is the Gran Hotel in Quito?)*

Now it's your turn! Put **hay** or **está** into the following sentences. You can also listen to the sentences on the CD. In these sentences prepositions are used in giving directions. At the right in the vocabulary box you will find some more prepositions that are useful in talking about places.

1. En el centro _____ la plaza mayor.

2. Enfrente de la iglesia _____ un edificio muy antiguo.

3. A la derecha de la iglesia _____ el museo de Arte Moderno.

4. Detrás del museo _____ una oficina de Correos.

> **¡Bueno saber!**
> **Hay** *(there is)* is also used before nouns without an article, before indefinite quantities, and before numbers.
> **¿Dónde hay vasos y platos?**
> **En México hay mucho tráfico.**
> **En esta ciudad hay cuatro teatros.**

> Prepositions:
> **a la derecha de** – *to the right of*
> **a la izquierda de** – *to the left of*
> **enfrente de** – *across from, facing*
> **detrás de** – *behind*
> **delante de** – *in front of*
> **sobre** – *on*
> **en** – *in* (**La iglesia está en la ciudad.**) *on* (**El teatro está en la plaza.**)
> **encima de** – *on top of*
> **debajo de** – *under*
> **al lado de** – *beside*
> **entre** – *between, among*
> **cerca de** – *near*
> **lejos de** – *far (away) from*

*ir + preposition—**ser** and **estar***

9

If you want to specify which means of transportation you use for traveling, you can use **ir** + **en** + the means of transportation:

> **ir en autobús** *(to take the bus)*
> **ir en motocicleta** *(to go by motorcycle)*

There are two exceptions: **ir a pie** *(to walk/go by foot)* and **ir a caballo** *(to go by horse).*

Now it's your turn! Write **en** or **a** in the following sentences.

1. ¿Cómo va Luis al trabajo? Luis va _____ metro.

2. ¿Cómo van Ángel y Carmen a casa? Ellos van _____ coche.

3. ¿Cómo van a la discoteca? Vamos _____ pie.

4. Nosotros vamos al trabajo _____ bicicleta o _____ autobús.

10

Write the correct forms of the verbs **ser** or **estar** in the blanks.

1. Hoy yo _____ muy bien.

2. Valentina _____ en Zaragoza.

3. Luis _____ muy enfermo.

4. Ángel _____ muy moreno.

5. Cecilia _____ mexicana.

6. Carmen y Ángel _____ en el centro de la ciudad.

7. Valentina _____ la hermana de Luis.

8. Carmen, ¿cómo _____?

11

Read the following plans for the future. Choose the correct term. You can also listen to the sentences on the CD.

1. Este año nosotros *van a pasar / vamos a pasar / va a cantar* quince días en Mallorca.
2. Yo *voy a hacer / voy a / va a tomar* un curso de español en Latinoamérica.
3. Valentina *vamos a viajar / va a escuchar / va a viajar* a Ecuador en septiembre.
4. Carmen y Ángel *vamos a pasear / van a pasear / vais a pasear* por el centro de la ciudad.
5. ¿Vosotros *van a dormir / voy a cantar / vais a comer* al restaurante Don Pepito?
6. Mañana *voy a empezar / voy a nadar / voy a comer* a estudiar.

12

Look at the illustrations and write the conjugated form of the verbs **ser** or **estar** in the blanks.

1. Miriam _____ muy enferma. Tiene un resfriado terrible.

2. Las niñas _____ guapísimas con estos uniformes de colegio.

3. Ustedes _____ Ignacio y Manuela, ¿verdad?

4. Él _____ el abuelo de Jorge, el niño que está al lado de la piscina.

13 ✎

Look at the illustrations and choose the appropriate answers. Only one of the answers is correct.

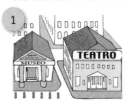

a. El museo está a la derecha del teatro.
b. El museo está enfrente del teatro.
c. El museo está a la izquierda del teatro.

a. Correos está al lado de la farmacia.
b. Correos está entre la farmacia y la policía.
c. Correos está al lado del parque.

a. La ópera está al lado del teatro.
b. La ópera está enfrente del estadio.
c. La ópera está en la calle Mayor.

a. El restaurante está lejos de la calle Mayor.
b. El restaurante está enfrente de la farmacia.
c. El restaurante está en el estadio.

a. La iglesia está en la plaza de la ciudad.
b. La iglesia está al lado del restaurante.
c. La iglesia está en el parque.

hay and *está/n*—*Prepositions*

1 ✏

Write the missing terms in the blanks. Pay close attention to the articles.
Which is appropriate: **está/n** or **hay**?

1. En Barcelona _____ una plaza muy grande.

2. ¿Dónde _____ el Museo de Arte Reina Sofía?

   ¿En Madrid o Barcelona?

3. Las casas del arquitecto Antonio Gaudí _____ en Barcelona.

4. En mi ciudad _____ muchas casas antiguas y muy bonitas.

2 ✏

Look at the illustrations and write the correct preposition in the spaces.

1. Miguel va al trabajo

   _____ moto.

2. Manuel y Gaby van al curso de

   español _____ bicicleta.

3. Nosotros siempre vamos

   _____ pie al gimnasio.

4. En Buenos Aires muchas personas

   van al centro _____ metro.

Prepositions

3 ✎

Read the questions and expressions. Which situation is appropriate to each illustration?

■ a. El parque está a la izquierda del museo.
■ b. El parque está detrás del museo.
■ c. El parque está a la derecha del museo.

■ a. El cine está en la plaza.
■ b. El cine está lejos de la plaza.
■ c. El cine está detrás de la plaza.

■ a. Correos está a la derecha del mercado.
■ b. Correos está entre la ópera y el cine.
■ c. Correos está al lado de la farmacia.

■ a. El teatro está en la plaza.
■ b. El teatro está entre el supermercado y el museo.
■ c. El teatro está lejos del museo.

4 ✎

Answer the questions and choose the appropriate answer. There is only one correct answer.

1. ¿Cómo va Valentina a la Universidad?

■ a. Va a pie.
■ b. Va al coche.
■ c. Ve el caballo.

2. ¿A dónde vamos a comer?

■ a. Vamos en avión.
■ b. Vamos a un restaurante.
■ c. Vamos en coche.

3. ¿Cómo van los pasajeros de Lufthansa?

■ a. Van en barco.
■ b. Van a pie.
■ c. Van en avión.

4. ¿A dónde vas en las vacaciones?

■ a. Voy a Mallorca.
■ b. Estoy en Mallorca.
■ c. Voy en autobús.

*The verbs **gustar**, **interesar**, and **encantar***

1

Read the dialogue between Valentina and her Argentine friend, Miguel.
You can also listen to the dialogue on the CD.

Valentina:	¿Estas vacaciones vas a visitar a tu familia a Buenos Aires?
Miguel:	No, prefiero visitar a mi familia en Navidad. Voy a estar aquí, en Madrid, para estudiar. Y tú, ¿qué vas a hacer?
Valentina:	Voy a ir a Ecuador en agosto. Me gusta mucho viajar y creo que es un país precioso. Además, me interesan mucho las culturas indígenas y me gustan mucho sus costumbres. En julio voy a trabajar para poder pagar el viaje y después, en agosto, de vacaciones.
Miguel:	¿Dónde vas a trabajar?
Valentina:	Voy a trabajar en un despacho de abogados. Estudio Derecho. Con este trabajo puedo practicar un poco y además ganar dinero. Y tú, ¿qué vas a hacer aquí? ¿sólo estudiar?
Miguel:	No, ya sabes que me gusta mucho jugar al fútbol. Además, me interesa aprender a jugar al tenis. Espero poder tomar unas clases. Y toco la guitarra. Toco con un grupo y tenemos que ensayar para un concierto en otoño.
Valentina:	¡Qué sorpresa! ¿Qué tipo de música hacéis?
Miguel:	Música latina.
Valentina:	Me encanta la música latina. Espero que me invites a tu concierto…
Miguel:	Claro que sí. Ya estás invitada…

visitar – *to visit*
gustar – *to like*
creer – *to believe*
precioso – *beautiful*
las culturas indígenas – *the native cultures*
interesar – *to interest*
pagar – *to pay*
el despacho de abogados – *the lawyers' office*
practicar – *to practice*
ganar dinero – *to earn money*
jugar – *to play*
tomar – *to take*
el otoño – *the fall*
¡qué sorpresa! – *what a surprise!*
invitar - *to invite*

*The verb **gustar***

2

Read these statements. Try to divide the expression into the following two categories: How many things do the various people like? One (1) or more (2+) things? You can also listen to the sentences on the CD.

1. A Valentina le gusta el chocolate. _____
2. A Valentina le gustan los bombones. _____
3. A Luis le gusta el fútbol. _____
4. A Luis le gustan los deportes. _____
5. A Carmen y a Ángel les gusta el teatro. _____
6. A Carmen y a Ángel les gustan los espectáculos. _____
7. A mí me gusta el trabajo en grupo. _____
8. A mí me gustan los trabajos en grupo. _____
9. A nosotros nos gusta la montaña más que la playa. _____
10. A nosotros nos gustan las montañas más que las playas. _____

gustar – *to like, be pleasing, taste good*
los bombones – *the bonbons*
el deporte – *the sport*
el espectáculo – *the performance*
la infusión – *herbal tea*
la montaña – *the mountain(s)*

¡Bueno saber!

The verbs **encantar** (*to love*), **interesar** (*to interest*), and **fascinar** (*to fascinate*) are often used instead of **gustar**. **Me encantan las flores.** (*I love flowers.*) **A Carolina le interesan las películas.** (*Carolina is interested in movies.*) **Nos fascina el mar.** (*The sea fascinates us.*) The indirect object pronouns are always placed immediately before the verb: **Me gusta vivir en Bolivia.** The negative element is placed before the pronouns: **No me gusta la cerveza caliente.**

3

The verb **gustar** is used in combination with a pronoun. Here are the non-accentuating indirect object pronouns:

me	*to / for me*
te	*to / for you*
le	*to / for him/ her/you (singular, formal)*
nos	*to / for us*
os	*to / for you (plural, familiar; Spain)*
les	*to / for them (m. or f.), you (plural, formal or informal)*

Also note the verb **gustar**. When is it used in the singular, and in the plural?

Singular: when one thing (**el chocolate** – *chocolate*) or one activity (**nadar** – *swimming*) is pleasing.

Plural: when several things are pleasing (**los bombones** – *the bonbons*).

 **amazon**.com.
Amazon.com
1850 Mercer Rd.
Lexington, KY 40511

Dr. Esmail Koushanpour
231 Ambria Dr
Mundelein, IL 60060–4811
United States

DL2DMHqpR/–1 of 1–/std–us/3555767 L

	Item Price	Total
HIPMENT		
ng with Spanish **Grammar: Easy Learning Step By Step with** ompact Disc (**Succeeding With Grammar Series**)	$13.25	$13.25
Maria Suarez ––– Paperback		
**) 0764193414		
414		

Subtotal	$13.25
Shipping & Handling	$3.99
Order Total	$17.24
Paid via Mastercard	$17.24
Balance due	$0.00

nt completes your order.

amazon.com.

Billing Address:
Dr. Esmail Koushanpour
231 Ambria Dr
Mundelein, IL 60060-4811
United States

Your order of Dec

Qty.	Item
	IN THIS
	Succeed
	Audio (
1	Lasierra,
	(** E-10
	0764193

This shipm

50/D

4

Now it's your turn! Match up the pronouns with the following sentences.

> os gustan – me gusta – le gusta – nos gustan

1. _____ la música latina. *(I)*

2. Los pueblos pequeños _____ mucho. *(we)*

3. A José _____ nadar en el mar. *(he)*

4. ¿_____ las culturas indígenas? *(you, pl., fam.)*

5

Match the statements on the left with the corresponding expressions on the right. On the left, possessive adjectives are used, but on the right, indirect objects with the verb *to like*.

1. Mi deporte favorito es el tenis.

2. Sus flores preferidas son las de color amarillo.

3. Tu color preferido es el azul.

4. Nuestros libros favoritos son las novelas.

5. Vuestro número preferido es el 9.

6. Su coche favorito es el A4.

a. A vosotros os gusta el número 9.

b. A ti te gusta el color azul.

c. A nosotros nos gustan las novelas.

d. A ellos les gusta el coche A4.

e. A mí me gusta el tenis.

f. A ella le gustan las flores amarillas.

*Indirect Object Pronouns—the Verb **querer***

6

Accentuating indirect object pronouns:

▶ § 27 Indirect Object
Pronouns

a mí	*to me*
a ti	*to you*
a él, a ella, a usted	*to him, her, you (formal)*
a nosotros / -as	*to us (m./f.)*
a vosotros / -as	*to you (pl., m./f., informal; Spain)*
a ellos / -as, a ustedes	*to them (m./f., to you, formal or informal)*

The accentuating indirect object pronouns (**a mí**, **a ti**, etc.) can be used in addition to the non-accentuating pronouns (**me**, **te**, etc.) in order to avoid misunderstandings or to place particular emphasis on a person.

But be careful: an accentuating pronoun (or indirect object) can not be used without a non-accentuating pronoun:

(**A él**) **le** gusta el mar, pero (**a mí**) no **me** gustan las olas.

7

Write the accentuating indirect object pronouns in the following sentences. You can also listen to these sentences on the CD.

1. _____ me gusta mucho ver la televisión.

2. _____ le encanta el trabajo en grupo.

3. _____ nos interesa la política.

4. _____ les encantan los perros.

8

The verb **querer** is irregular. Pay close attention to the forms.

e ▶ ie	**querer** *(to want)*
yo	qui**e**ro
tú	qui**e**res
él, ella, usted	qui**e**re
nosotros / as	quer**emos**
vosotros / as	quer**éis**
ellos / as, ustedes	qui**e**ren

¡Bueno saber!

Querer is a verb from the group that has a spelling change form **e ▶ ie**.
This group also includes such verbs as **empezar** (*to begin*), **pensar** (*to think*), **sentir** (*to feel*), **perder** (*to lose*), **entender** (*to understand*), **preferir** (*to prefer*), etc. There are still a few additional groups that you will learn later.

9 ✏

Now it's your turn! Complete the sentences by writing the missing forms of the verb **querer** (*to want*) in the blanks.

1. Miguel no _____ jugar al tenis pero yo sí que _____

   jugar al tenis.

2. Nosotros _____ jugar a las cartas todos los domingos por la

   tarde en el casino.

3. Ustedes _____ jugar al golf desde hace mucho tiempo.

4. ¿Tú _____ jugar al fútbol con nosotros?

10 TR.25 👓

The verb **poder** (*to be able*) is irregular.
But this time it's not a verb that belongs to the **e ▶ ie** group.
This is a verb from the **o ▶ ue** group. The last vowel of the word stem changes when the stem is stressed.

▶ § 14 Irregular Verbs

Other verbs of this group are **costar** (*to cost*), **dormir** (*to sleep*), **mover** (*to move*), **acostarse** (*to lie down*), **volver** (*to come/go back*), **encontrar** (*to find, meet*), etc.

Read the forms of the verb **poder** and try to pronounce them. You can also listen to them on the CD.

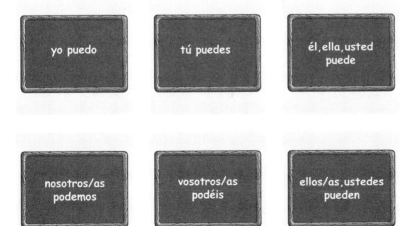

| yo puedo | tú puedes | él, ella, usted puede |
| nosotros/as podemos | vosotros/as podéis | ellos/as, ustedes pueden |

Irregular Verbs

11

With some verbs, only the first person singular is irregular. All other persons follow the pattern of the relevant conjugation:

	hacer	**salir**	**saber**
yo	**hago**	**salgo**	**sé**
tú	haces	sales	sabes
él, ella, usted	hace	sale	sabe
nosotros / as	hacemos	salimos	sabemos
vosotros / as	hacéis	salís	sabéis
ellos / as, ustedes	hacen	salen	saben

12

Now try to choose the correct verb and underline it.

1. Yo *salgo / salís / sale* mucho con mis amigos.
2. ¿*Sabéis / Sabemos / Sabe* usted dónde hay una farmacia por aquí?
3. Tú conoces el camino pero yo no *sabemos / sé / sabéis* como llegar.

13

▶ § 14 Irregular Verbs

Provide the indicated verb forms:

    a. 1. Person Singular from **saber**   _____

    b. 1. Person Singular from **traducir** _____

    c. 2. Person Plural from **querer**   _____

    d. 1. Person Plural from **dormir**   _____

    e. 2. Person Singular from **sentir**   _____

    f. 1. Person Singular from **poder**   _____

    g. 3. Person Plural from **pensar**   _____

    h. 1. Person Singular from **conocer** _____

    i. 3. Person Singular from **contar**   _____

14

Write the appropriate indirect object pronouns (**me**, **te**, **le**, **nos**, **os**, **les**) in the blanks.

1. A Alejandro _____ gusta comer patatas bravas.

2. A mí _____ encantan los niños.

3. A todo el mundo no _____ interesan las noticias deportivas.

4. A mis amigas y a mí _____ gustan las películas de terror.

5. A nadie _____ gusta estar de mal humor.

6. A ustedes _____ interesa demasiado mi vida privada.

7. A vosotras _____ encanta ir de vacaciones y viajar muy lejos.

8. A ti _____ gusta el café sin azúcar.

> **a todo el mundo –** *everyone*
> **a nadie** – *nobody*

15

Choose the correct answer. You can also listen to the questions on the CD.

1. ¿Qué color prefieres?
   - ☐ a. Prefiero el rojo.
   - ☐ b. Preferimos el rojo.
   - ☐ c. Prefieren el verde.

2. ¿Qué queréis hacer hoy?
   - ☐ a. Queréis ir al zoológico.
   - ☐ b. Queremos estar en casa.
   - ☐ c. Quieren cantar en el coro.

3. ¿Ustedes dónde piensan ir de vacaciones?
   - ☐ a. Piensan ir a Mallorca.
   - ☐ b. Pienso ir a América.
   - ☐ c. Pensamos ir a México.

4. ¿Cuándo empezáis el curso de español?
   - ☐ a. Empiezan en mayo.
   - ☐ b. Empezamos el curso en octubre.
   - ☐ c. Empiezo mañana.

5. ¿Qué bebida prefiere tu novia?
   - ☐ a. Prefiere el café al té.
   - ☐ b. Prefieren el café.
   - ☐ c. Prefiero un refresco.

6. ¿Cuándo empiezas a trabajar?
   - ☐ a. Empiezan la semana próxima.
   - ☐ b. Empieza el lunes.
   - ☐ c. Empiezo esta misma tarde.

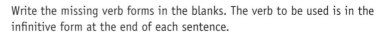

16

Write the missing verb forms in the blanks. The verb to be used is in the infinitive form at the end of each sentence.

1. Valentina _____ todo el día en su viaje. (pensar)

2. ¿Vosotros _____ dónde vive Cecilia? (saber)

3. Yo no _____ lo que dices. ¿Puedes hablar más despacio, por favor? (entender)

4. ¿Qué _____ tomar, un café o un té? (querer)

5. Nosotros cocinamos y ellos _____ la mesa. (poner)

6. ¿Dónde está? Yo no lo _____. (ver)

7. ¿Cómo _____ a casa, en taxi? (volver)

8. ¿Cuánto _____ las cebollas? (costar)

17 ✎

These sentences are mixed up. Put the words into the correct sequence.

1. vacaciones / encanta / en / me / a / mí / estudiar / las / .

_____

2. empresa / te / una / trabajar / gusta / internacional / en / ¿ / ?

_____

3. ellos / fiestas / a / les / pueblos / en / gustan / las / los / .

_____

4. a / gustan / nos / alemanes / Marta / y / coches / mí / a / los / .

_____

5. interesa / él / a / política / la / le / .

_____

6. jazz / ustedes / a / les / fascina / el / ¿ / ?

_____

1

Read the situations. Which situation matches each illustration? You can also listen to the sentences on the CD.

    a. Valentina vuelve a casa.
    b. Valentina come sopa.
    c. Valentina duerme mucho.

    a. Luis trabaja mucho.
    b. Luis duerme intensamente.
    c. Luis habla por teléfono.

    a. Él trabaja en una empresa.
    b. El hombre duerme en un hotel.
    c. Él quiere a su mujer.

    a. Juan puede hablar chino.
    b. Juan es tímido.
    c. Juan vive en Asturias.

    a. La chica piensa en su novio.
    b. La chica juega al tenis.
    c. La chica piensa en sus exámenes de matemáticas.

    a. A Miguel le gusta correr.
    b. A Miguel le gusta el vino.
    c. Miguel prefiere el deporte en equipo.

*Indirect Object Pronouns—the Verb **gustar***

2 ✏

Write the appropriate indirect object pronouns in the blanks.

1. A María _____ gusta el cine.

2. A ellos _____ interesa la economía.

3. A ti _____ encanta leer.

4. A nosotros _____ gusta comer comida de otros países.

3 ✏

Put the syllables into the correct sequence.

1. noz – co – co   _____

2. déis – po   _____

3. tís – sen   _____

4. za – em – pie   _____

5. fie – pre – res   _____

6. den – tien – en   _____

4 ✏

Answer the questions and choose the appropriate answer. There is just one correct answer.

1. ¿A quién le gusta ir al cine?
   - ▨ a. A José Luis le gusta ir al teatro.
   - ▨ b. A Mariana le gusta mucho ir al cine.
   - ▨ c. A mis padres les gusta estar siempre en casa.

2. ¿Les gustan los idiomas?
   - ▨ a. A nosotros nos gustan, pero no tenemos mucho tiempo para estudiar.
   - ▨ b. A ellos no les gustan otras lenguas.
   - ▨ c. Sí, a mí no y a ellos creo que tampoco les gusta la música.

3. ¿Les interesa la política?
   - ▨ a. A ti no te interesa nada la política.
   - ▨ b. A nosotros nos interesa muchísimo.
   - ▨ c. A vosotros os da igual.

Reflexive Verbs

1 TR.28

Today Valentina gets up early, for she has an important appointment.
Read the dialogue between Valentina and her mother. You can also
listen to the dialogue on the CD.

Carmen:	Hola Valentina. ¡Qué pronto te levantas!
Valentina:	Es que tengo una cita muy importante en el despacho.
Carmen:	¿Quieres desayunar conmigo?
Valentina:	Sí, pero primero voy a ducharme.
Carmen:	Yo ya pongo la mesa y hago el café.

> **el despacho** – *the office*
> **el caso** – *the case*
> **el cliente** – *the client*
> **la reunión** – *the meeting*
> **traer** – *to bring*
> **acordarse** – *to remember*

En el baño está el hermano de Valentina:

Valentina:	¿Te falta mucho?
Luis:	No lo sé, …, sólo me afeito, me lavo los dientes y me visto y ¡ya está!
Valentina:	Tengo mucha prisa.
Luis:	Ya lo veo, ¿por qué?
Valentina:	Tengo una reunión importante en el trabajo.

Durante el desayuno:

Carmen:	¿Con quién tienes esa reunión tan importante?
Valentina:	Con un cliente nuevo, ¿te acuerdas del caso «Pérez»?
Carmen:	Sí, me acuerdo.
Valentina:	Pues con el Sr. Pérez.
Carmen:	¡Qué interesante!
Valentina:	Sí, me interesa mucho el caso del Sr. Pérez y además gano el dinero para pagar las vacaciones…
Carmen:	¡Qué bien!
Luis:	Buenos días, ya estoy aquí, ¿traigo el café?
Valentina:	Por fin, me voy a duchar.

ducharse
yo me ducho
tú te duchas
él, ella, usted se ducha

2

Except for the presence of pronouns, reflexive verbs (which end in **-se**) behave like other verbs and correspond to one of three conjugation groups (**-ar**, **-er**, **-ir**). Many of these verbs also change their stem vowel:

acostarse: o ▸ ue, despertarse: e ▸ ie.

The reflexive pronouns generally come before the conjugated verb. With infinitives and present participles, they can also be attached.

Se quiere duchar. Quiere ducharse.

-gu- ▸ -g-
conseguir ▸ consigo
seguir ▸ sigo

Further Spanish reflexive verbs include **maquillarse** (*to put on makeup*), **peinarse** (*to comb one's hair*), **afeitarse** (*to shave*), **acostumbrarse** (*to get used to*), and others.

¡Bueno saber!

Careful! Some verbs are used reflexively in Spanish, but not in English: **acostarse** (*to go to bed, lie down*), **despertarse** (*to wake up*), **levantarse** (*to get up*), **llamarse** (*to be named*), etc.

Some verbs are used both reflexively and non-reflexively. Commonly the verbs have a different meaning in their reflexive form. Here are just a few examples:

abrir (*to open*)	**abrirse** (*to open up, expand*)
aburrir (*to bore*)	**aburrirse** (*to be bored*)
dormir (*to sleep*)	**dormirse** (*to fall asleep*)
llamar (*to call*)	**llamarse** (*to be named*)

3

Here are some actions and activities. Put the reflexive verbs into the blanks. You can also listen to the sentences on the CD.

> se lava – se acuestan – me despierto – os desvestís –
> se ducha – te levantas – nos vestimos

lavarse –
to wash up
vestirse –
to get dressed
desvestirse –
to get undressed

1. Yo _____ a las 7 de la mañana.

2. Tú _____ a las 8.15 de la mañana.

3. Usted _____ a las 9.30 de la mañana.

4. Ella _____ los dientes todos los días.

5. Nosotras _____ a las 10 de la mañana.

6. Niños, ahora vosotros _____ y os ponéis el pijama.

7. Ellos _____ a las 10 de la noche.

4

The Direct Object Pronouns:

me	*me*	**nos**	*us*
te	*you*	**os**	*you (familiar, pl., Spain)*
lo	*him, it, you*	**los, las**	*them, you*
la	*her, it, you*		

The direct object pronouns refer to something or someone that has already been mentioned.

Direct object pronouns agree in gender and number with the word to which they refer, and they always come immediately before the verb.

> **¿Lees <u>el periódico</u>? No, no <u>lo</u> leo.**
> *Do you read the newspaper? No, I don't read it.*

> **¡Bueno saber!**
> When the direct object comes before the verb, it must be repeated in the form of a direct object pronoun. This pronoun agrees in gender and number with the word to which it refers. **Las llaves las tengo yo.**
> *I have the keys.*

5

The questions in the pictures match one of the answers below. Match up the answers with the correct pictures.

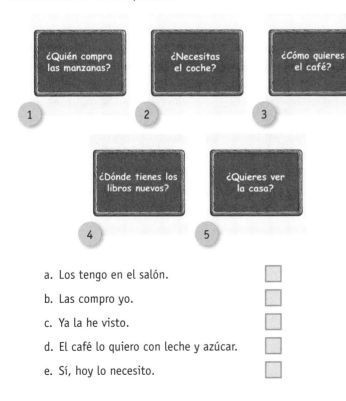

¿Quién compra las manzanas?	¿Necesitas el coche?	¿Cómo quieres el café?
1	2	3

¿Dónde tienes los libros nuevos?	¿Quieres ver la casa?
4	5

a. Los tengo en el salón. ☐

b. Las compro yo. ☐

c. Ya la he visto. ☐

d. El café lo quiero con leche y azúcar. ☐

e. Sí, hoy lo necesito. ☐

6

We know that with some verbs the stem vowel changes in forms where the stress falls on the word stem (in all persons except for **nosotros** and **vosotros**).

Here are a few more in the group **e ▶ i**

	pedir *(to order)*
yo	pido
tú	pides
él, ella, usted	pide
nosotros / as	pedimos
vosotros / as	pedís
ellos / as, ustedes	piden

This also applies to the following verbs: **conseguir** *(to obtain, get)*, **elegir** *(to choose, select)*, **freír** *(to fry)*, **repetir** *(to repeat)*, **seguir** *(to follow, continue)*, **servir** *(to serve)*, **vestir** *(to dress, wear)*.

With the verbs **seguir**, **conseguir**, and **elegir**, you also have to keep in mind that the 1st person singular form is spelled differently, in order to preserve the pronunciation.

-gu- > -g-
conseguir > consigo
seguir > sigo

- g - > - j -
elegir > elijo

7

Now it's your turn. Put the verbs into the sentences.

> eliges – pide – consigue – sigue

1. Valentina le _____ el coche a su madre.

2. Él normalmente _____ todo lo que quiere.

3. ¿Qué revistas _____?

4. _____ todo recto por esta calle y verás la iglesia.

8

Some irregular verbs have both a stem change and an irregular first person singular:

decir: **digo**, di**c**es, di**c**e, decimos, decís, di**c**en
tener: **tengo**, t**ie**nes, t**ie**ne, tenemos, tenéis, t**ie**nen
venir: **vengo**, v**ie**nes, v**ie**ne, venimos, venís, v**ie**nen

Write in the spaces the appropriate conjugated form of the verbs at the end of the sentences.

1. Ella _____ 32 años. (tener)

2. Ellos _____ que la ciudad es muy bonita. (decir)

3. ¿Tú _____ de Barcelona o de Madrid? (venir)

> **¡Bueno saber!**
> The following verbs are totally irregular:
> **ser** *(to be)*: soy, eres, es, somos, sois, son
> **estar** *(to be)*: estoy, estás, está, estamos, estáis, están
> **ir** *(to go)*: voy, vas, va, vamos, vais, van
> **haber** *(the helping verb to have)*: he, has, ha, hemos, habéis, han

9

Write the missing reflexive verbs in the appropriate conjugated forms in the spaces.

> despertarse – lavarse – acostarse – levantarse – llamarse – ducharse

1. Valentina _____ a las siete de la mañana.

2. Yo _____ después de desayunar.

3. Nosotros _____ muy tarde.

4. Luis y Alicia _____ para hacer la siesta todos los domingos.

5. Vosotras _____ Isabel y Encarna.

6. Tú _____ los dientes muy mal.

10

Which verb doesn't belong? Underline it.

1. pido / vengo /voy / dices
2. vamos / tenemos / repetís / elegimos
3. eliges / vienes / consigues / está
4. vienen / digo / tienen / son
5. repite / consigues / pides / vas
6. venís / conseguís / decís / eligen

11 ✐

Write the appropriate conjugated verb forms in the spaces.

> traducir – tener – costar – jugar – poder – entender

1. En la oficina yo _____ muchos documentos del inglés al español.

2. ¿Tú _____ pasar por la casa de Valentina esta tarde?

3. Yo no _____ nada. Habla más despacio, por favor.

4. ¿Cuánto _____ los tomates?

5. _____ 25 años, ¿y tú?

6. Normalmente ellos _____ al tenis todos los lunes.

12 ✐

Read the questions and answer them. (**¿Usted compra los tomates en la verdulería? Sí, los compro en la verdulería.**) Use the pronouns that stand for direct object nouns (**lo**, **la**, **los**, or **las**)

1. ¿Usted compra los libros en la librería?

_____

2. ¿Tú vas a ver a Juana?

_____

3. Gabriel compra el pan, ¿verdad?

_____

4. ¿Usted quiere las revistas de moda?

_____

5. Prefieres los vinos de Chile, ¿verdad?

_____

Reflexive and Irregular Verbs

13 🖉

Complete the sentences with the appropriate reflexive verbs.

▶ § 21 Reflexive Verbs

1. Él _____ en diez minutos. (afeitarse)

2. Yo siempre _____ a todo rápidamente. (adaptarse)

3. Creo que ustedes _____ demasiado. (preocuparse)

4. Eva y yo _____ muchas veces en la calle. (encontrarse)

5. Sus amigos no _____ a decirle nada. (atreverse)

6. Ustedes _____ muy bien, ¿verdad? (llevarse)

14 🖉

Put the appropriate verb forms into the blanks.

quieren – podéis – van – quieres – va – pueden – vais

1. Vosotros, ¿a qué hora _____ al cine?

2. Chicos, ¿_____ llamar a Chema, por favor?

3. ¿Tu hija _____ a la universidad?

4. Si ustedes _____, _____ ver el piso hoy.

5. ¿_____ ustedes al Retiro?

6. ¿_____ tomar algo, Noelia?

Direct Object Pronouns

15 🖉

These sentences are scrambled. Put the individual words back into the correct sequence. Pay particular attention to the position of the pronouns.

1. gusta / a / me / televisión / la / mí / .

   _____

2. ver / quiero / te / .

   _____

3. lo / me / dices / .

   _____

4. Valentina / hablar / a / encanta / le / .

   _____

5. me / no / a / importa / mí / .

   _____

6. hacerlo / puedo / no / .

   _____

7. los / supermercado / compro / el / en / .

   _____

8. por / la / teléfono / llamo / .

   _____

16 🖉

Plug in the direct object pronouns.

1. ¿Dónde está la revista? No _____ veo.

2. No veo las gafas. ¿_____ tienes tú?

3. Yo no tengo los 20 pesos. _____ tiene tu hermano.

4. ¿Dónde está el bolso? No _____ veo.

5. ¿Tienes tú las cosas? Yo no _____ tengo.

1

Write the missing conjugated verb forms in the blanks. The verbs are indicated at the end of the sentences.

1. ¿Cuánto _____ el pan? (costar)

2. ¿_____ tú tiempo mañana para ir al cine? (tener)

3. Yo no _____ mis llaves. ¿Dónde estarán? (encontrar)

4. Yo soy de Hermosillo, ¿y tú, de dónde _____? (ser)

5. Nosotros _____ el vino tinto, ¿y ustedes? (preferir)

6. Yo no _____ dónde está la iglesia. ¿Tú lo sabes? (saber)

2 TR.30

Which statement goes with each illustration? Choose the appropriate answer. You can also listen to the statements on the CD.

a. Me levanto a las ocho de la mañana.
b. Siempre me ducho con agua fría.
c. Me visto con mucha tranquilidad.

a. Juan se despierta a las siete y media de la mañana.
b. Él se peina y se afeita.
c. Se ducha con agua caliente.

a. Valentina se acuesta muy tarde.
b. Todos los días se lava los dientes.
c. Ella se viste.

a. Valentina se despierta a las ocho.
b. Ella se maquilla en el baño.
c. Se mira horas y horas en el espejo.

Direct Object Pronouns—Present Tense

3 ✎

Write the appropriate direct object pronouns in the following sentences.

1. ¿Dónde compras los plátanos?

   _____ compro en el super-mercado.

2. ¿Conoces a María?

   Sí, _____ conozco.

3. ¿Lees este libro?

   No, no _____ leo.

4. ¿Invitas a tus amigas a la cena?

   Sí, _____ invito.

4 ✎

Write in the spaces the present tense of the indicated verbs.

1. 1ª persona del singular del verbo **ser**.   _____

2. 1ª persona del plural del verbo **lavarse**.   _____

3. 3ª persona del plural del verbo **decir**.   _____

4. 2ª persona del singular del verbo **jugar**.   _____

5. 2ª persona del plural del verbo **acostarse**.   _____

6. 2ª persona del singular del verbo **hacer**.   _____

7. 1ª persona del singular del verbo **venir**.   _____

8. 3ª persona del plural del verbo **ir**.   _____

9. 1ª persona de plural del verbo **estar**.   _____

10. 2ª persona del plural del verbo **decir**.   _____

11. 1ª persona del singular del verbo **tener**.   _____

12. 3ª persona del singular del verbo **despertarse**.   _____

Estar + *Present Participle*

1

There is a **concierto al aire libre** (*an outdoor concert*). Read what the people are doing at this concert. Match the sentences with the translations. You can also listen to the sentences on the CD.

1. ¿Qué está haciendo el público?
   El público está aplaudiendo.

2. ¿Qué canción están cantando?
   Los cantantes están cantando una canción moderna.

3. ¿Qué está haciendo el periodista?
   El periodista está escribiendo notas.

4. ¿Qué están mirando los fotógrafos?
   No están mirando, están fotografiando.

5. ¿Cómo está tocando la orquesta?
   La orquesta está tocando muy bien.

a. *How is the band playing?*

   The band is playing very well.

b. *What is the journalist doing?*
   The journalist is writing notes.

c. *What is the audience doing?*

   The audience is clapping.

d. *Which song are they singing?*

   The vocalists are singing a contemporary song.

e. *What are the photographers looking at?*
   The photographers are not looking; they are taking photographs.

▶ § 18 The Present Participle / Form and Usage

Formation and Use of the Present Participle

2

The structure **estar** + present participle is used to describe an action that is currently going on:

estoy comiendo *(I am eating)*

The present participle is very easy to construct from the infinitive:
Verbs ending in **-ar** change their ending to **-ando**;
Verbs ending in **-er** and **-ir** change their ending to **-iendo**:

trabajar	▸	trabajando
comer	▸	comiendo
vivir	▸	viviendo

With infinitives and imperative forms, the pronoun must be attached to the verb; otherwise it must come before the verb. With the present participle both forms exist.

When the sentence contains a pronoun, it either comes before the verb **estar** or is attached to the present participle. In this case an accent is required to preserve the stress:

Me lo está diciendo. – Está diciéndomelo. *(He is telling me it.)*

3 ✏

Now it's your turn! Choose the correct answer. Refer to the two illustrations.

1. Valentina está *estudiando / bailando / hablando por teléfono*.

2. Miguel está *corriendo / bebiendo un café / hablando por teléfono*.

Estar + *Present Participle*

4

Read the dialogue between Miguel, an Argentine friend of Valentina's, and Valentina. They are in Valentina's house, where they are organizing their photo album. You can also listen to the dialogue on the CD.

Miguel: ¡Hola Valentina! ¿Qué estás haciendo?
Valentina: Estoy ordenando las fotos de este año. He hecho muchas fotos y estoy clasificándolas.
Miguel: ¿De dónde son estas fotos tan divertidas?
Valentina: Son de la boda de mi primo. ¿Has estado alguna vez en una boda española?
Miguel: No, nunca he estado en ninguna boda aquí. Estoy esperando la celebración de tu boda.
Valentina: ¿Qué? Creo que vas a tener que esperar mucho tiempo.
Miguel: ¿Por qué has hecho este año tantas fotos?
Valentina: Siempre hago muchas fotos, la fotografía me encanta. Especialmente este año he viajado mucho y he conocido a mucha gente y muchos lugares. ¡Mira! Éstas son de mi viaje en bicicleta por el Camino de Santiago. ¿Las quieres ver?
Miguel: Éstas ya las conozco. Pero me las puedes enseñar de nuevo, son muy bonitas.
Valentina: Tengo muchas más, mira estas otras son de mi viaje a Ecuador. ¿Te acuerdas?, este verano he estado en Ecuador. Este viaje te lo recomiendo.
Miguel: Yo ya he visitado Ecuador. Aunque no he estado nunca en las Islas Galápagos.
Valentina: ¿Tienes ganas de ir de vacaciones conmigo? Estoy planeando un viaje a Cuba, pero un viaje interesante, nada de turismo de masas.
Miguel: Voy a pensármelo. Depende de mis exámenes.
Valentina: Tú y tus exámenes...
Miguel: Tú y tus viajes...

ordenar – *organize, arrange*
clasificar – *to sort*
divertido/a – *funny*
la boda – *the wedding*
el primo – *the cousin*
la celebración – *the celebration*
especialmente – *especially*
el lugar – *the place*
¡mira! – *look!*
la bicicleta – *the bicycle*
el Camino de Santiago – *a pilgrimage route*
enseñar – *to show*
recomendar – *o recommend*
el turismo de masas – *mass tourism*

▶ § 15 The Present
Perfect Tense
Formation + Usage

desayunar –
to have breakfast
el cine – *the movie*
el extranjero – *overseas*
**las Cataratas del
Iguazú** – *the Iguazú Falls*
la leche – *milk*
la tostada – *toast*
el menú del día –
the daily menu
el tráfico – *the traffic*
la esquina – *the corner*

5

The questions on the left don't match up with the answers on the right. Match them up with the terms. Do you recognize a past-tense form here?

1. ¿Dónde han estado de
vacaciones este verano?
2. ¿Qué película ha visto en el
cine hoy?
3. ¿Has trabajado alguna vez en
el extranjero?
4. ¿Con quién has ido al teatro?
5. ¿En qué supermercado han
comprado?
6. ¿Por qué han llegado tan tarde?

a. En las Cataratas del Iguazú.
b. No, nunca.
c. El Señor de los Anillos.
d. Por el tráfico.
e. En el supermercado de la
esquina.
f. Con Susana.

¡Bueno saber!
The present perfect
tense is also used with
events for which the
time of occurrence is
not specified or not
important, for example,
alguna vez *(once)*,
todavía no *(not yet)*,
muchas veces *(often)*,
nunca *(never)*, **ya**
(already).

6

The present perfect tense is a past-tense form that is also used with time expressions that have a connection to the present: **hoy** *(today)*, **esta mañana** *(this morning)*, **esta semana** *(this week)*, **este verano** *(this summer)*, **este año** *(this year)*.

The present perfect tense consists of two parts: the present-tense form of **haber** + the past participle of the verb (invariable); for example, **he trabajado** *(I worked / have worked / did work)*.
Verbs ending in **-ar** (for example, **trabajar**) form their past participle in the ending **-ado** (for example, **trabajado**).

Verbs ending in **-er** and **-ir** (for example, **comer**, **vivir**) form their past participle with the ending **-ido** (**comido**, **vivido**).
The present tense of **haber**: **he**, **has**, **ha**, **hemos**, **habéis**, **han**

José was invited to a wedding. Match up the verbs with the sentences.

> hemos comido – se ha casado – ha sido – ha habido – ha llevado

1. Un compañero _____.

2. La boda _____ hoy por la mañana en la Iglesia
de San Lorenzo.

3. La novia _____ un traje blanco precioso.

4. _____ muchos invitados.

5. _____ en un restaurante buenísimo.

7 👓 ✏️

In the following text you will find some verbs with other past participles that you probably don't yet know; they are irregular. Try to determine which verbs these participles come from. Valentina is telling her friend Cecilia what it was like in the discotheque this evening.

Hemos **vuelto** a salir esta noche y hemos **ido** a una discoteca. La discoteca ha **abierto** a las diez de la noche. Allí hemos **visto** a muchos conocidos de la facultad. No nos han **puesto** problemas a la entrada y han **sido** muy amables con nosotras. ¿Te he **dicho** lo que hemos **tomado**? Hemos **bebido** un cóctel exótico buenísimo. Te he **escrito** la dirección de esta discoteca en este papel.

Well? Did you notice which irregularities came up in the present perfect? Put the past participles into the blanks.

> puesto – abierto – visto – vuelto

1. La discoteca ha _____ hoy a las 10 de noche.

2. Hemos _____ a muchos amigos.

3. Mis amigos han _____ a salir esta noche.

4. Ustedes han _____ muchos problemas en la entrada.

> ### ¡Bueno saber!
>
> Irregular Past Participle Forms:
> **abrir** ▸ **abierto** *(open)*
> **decir** ▸ **dicho** *(said)*
> **escribir** ▸ **escrito** *(written)*
> **hacer** ▸ **hecho** *(done, made)*
> **ir** ▸ **ido** *(gone)*
> **poner** ▸ **puesto** *(put, placed)*
> **ver** ▸ **visto** *(seen)*
> **volver** ▸ **vuelto** *(returned)*

8 👓

No can mean *no* or *not*. It always comes before the verb. The present perfect is constructed using the present tense of the verb **haber** + the past participle. The forms of the verb **haber** are always placed directly before the helping verb.

Hoy **he comido** mucho.
Hoy **no he comido** mucho.

9

Put the following words into the blanks.

> no – ningún – nadie – nada

1. Esta mañana no he estudiado _____ .

2. Cuando paseo por el parque nunca veo a _____ animal.

3. He tenido una visita y _____ he podido hacer todas mis cosas.

4. En toda la semana no ha venido _____ a comprar.

10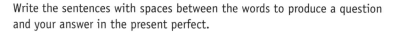

When a pronoun – whether direct, indirect, or reflexive—is used with a verb in the present perfect tense, it comes immediately before the verb:

- **¿Has leído el periódico hoy?**
  Have you read the newspaper today?
- **Sí, lo he leído.**
  Yes, I have read it.

When direct and indirect object pronouns occur together, the indirect comes before the direct.

> **Si no lo has leído, te lo leo yo.**
> *If you haven't read it, I will read it to you.*

The indirect object pronouns **le / les** change to **se** when followed by the direct object pronouns **lo / la / los / las**:

> **Se lo he leído yo.**
> *I read it to him.*

11

Write the sentences with spaces between the words to produce a question and your answer in the present perfect.

1. ¿HasvistoaAna?Sí,lahevisto.

   _____

2. ¿Sehanduchadoestamañana?Sí,sehanduchado.

   _____

3. ¿Telohadicho?No,nomelohadicho.

   _____

12 ✎

Look at the illustrations and choose the appropriate answer to the question
What is s/he doing?

1. ▢ a. Está jugando al tenis.
   ▢ b. Está leyendo el periódico.
   ▢ c. Está comiendo.

2. ▢ a. Está leyendo un libro.
   ▢ b. Está trabajando.
   ▢ c. Está durmiendo.

3. ▢ a. Está hablando con su televisión.
   ▢ b. Está hablando por teléfono.
   ▢ c. Está cantando una opera.

4. ▢ a. Se está bañando.
   ▢ b. Se está lavando los dientes.
   ▢ c. Se está duchando.

13 ✎

Today was Valentina's birthday, and she tells us what she did. Complete the
sentences with the correct verbs. Pay attention to the reflexive verbs!

1. Hoy _____ pronto para preparar una cena muy

   especial. (levantarse)

2. _____ la casa. (decorar)

3. _____ a mis amigos por teléfono. (invitar)

4. Después _____ y _____ con

   un traje nuevo precioso. (bañarse, vestirse)

5. La fiesta _____ un éxito. (ser)

6. _____ muy tarde. (acostarse)

7. _____ un día muy especial. (ser)

14

Read the participle that is used to form the present perfect tense. Try to place the terms into the categories of regular or irregular participles. You can also listen to the participles on the CD.

> vivido – puesto – querido – abierto – leído – ido – comido – hecho – bailado – vuelto – jugado – visto

Regular Participles	Irregular Participles

15

In the strings of letters below try to identify the direct object to which the corresponding pronoun refers. Underline it.

1. Lo ha visto en el fútbol.
   msdfraljugadormndsff

2. Se la ha comido muy deprisa.
   kksldlatartadechocolatemsdkdd

3. Los hemos invitado a cenar.
   anuestrosamigosalkjdsfuajdsfo

4. Lo estoy viendo desde mi ventana.
   gsjdlfelconciertomajdhdu

5. Las hemos comprado en la floristería.
   shdieolflflrplasrosas

6. Las hemos conocido en París.
   Ajsklslalasfrancesasmcisdofl

Present Participle—The Present Perfect Tense—Pronouns

1

Look at the illustrations and write what the people are doing.

1. Ella _____
   al dominó.

2. Ellos _____
   por el parque.

3. Tú _____
   en una fiesta.

4. Yo _____
   un libro muy
   interesante.

2

Write the missing verbs in the present perfect tense in the spaces.

1. Primera persona del singular del verbo **volver**   _____

2. Primera persona del plural del verbo **cantar**   _____

3. Segunda persona del singular del verbo **poner**   _____

4. Segunda persona del plural del verbo **decir**   _____

5. Tercera persona del singular del verbo **hacer**   _____

6. Tercera persona del plural del verbo **abrir**   _____

3

Look at the sentences. Which pronoun is correct?

1. Se *lo / le / la* he dicho a Juan. (el comentario)

2. *Lo / La / Le* miro y me gusta el contraste. (la foto)

3. *Le / La / Lo* ha estado bailando otra vez. (el tango)

4. *Le / Lo / La* he escrito una carta de amor. (a él/a ella)

5. *Las / Los / Les* ha cuidado mucho. (a los niños)

6. *Los / Las / Les* ha querido siempre. (a las niñas)

7. *Les / Los / Las* ha dicho la verdad. (a ellos/a ellas)

The Present Perfect

4 _✎_

Match up the questions and the answers. For each question there are two possible answers. Put the number of the question into the appropriate boxes by the questions.

1. ¿Te ha gustado la película?	▦ a. No, no me ha gustado nada.
	▦ b. Sí, tenemos uno.
2. ¿Ha estado alguna vez en Chile?	▦ c. No, no he estado nunca.
	▦ d. Sí, me ha gustado mucho.
3. ¿Tienen algún amigo en Guatemala?	▦ e. Sí, he estado muchas veces.
	▦ f. No, no tenemos ninguno.

5 _✎_

Underline the term that doesn't belong with the others.

1. he vuelto – han ido – ha vuelto – hemos vuelto

2. jugando – cantando – riendo – hacer

3. visto – dicho – cantando – abierto

4. la – lo – las – sus

5. he – somos – has – ha

6. abro – abres – abre – ha abierto

7. ir – hablar – comer – estudiando

8. leer – estar cantando – estar riendo – estar jugando

9. he puesto – he dicho – ha puesto – habéis puesto

10. estoy – estás – está – estando

11. me – mis – te – se

12. hemos jugado – hemos buscado – hemos leído – habéis ido

1

Read the questions and answers. Note that the verbs are in a new past-tense form. Match up the questions and the answers. You can also listen to them on the CD.

1. ¿Dónde naciste?

2. ¿En qué ciudad estudiaste?

3. ¿Cuándo te casaste?

4. ¿Dónde viviste en el año 1996?

5. ¿Cuándo escribiste una carta de amor por última vez?

a. Nací en Zaragoza.

b. Escribí una carta de amor por última vez en el año 1999.

c. Estudio todavía en Madrid.

d. No estoy casada.

e. Viví en Madrid.

◀ **nacer** –
to be born
la ciudad – *the city*
casarse – *to get married*
la carta de amor –
the love letter

2

Read the sentences. They will provide you with more information about Miguel's past. Match up the following infinitives with the verbs in bold print. You can also listen to the sentences on the CD.

> aprender – viajar – jugar – conocer – estudiar

1. Miguel **estudió** en España. Nunca ha estudiado francés. _____

2. El año pasado él **viajó** por Europa. Este año no ha viajado todavía a Argentina. _____

3. De niño Miguel **jugó** mucho al fútbol. Siempre ha jugado mucho con la pelota. _____

4. Miguel **conoció** a una española en la Argentina. Esta mañana ha conocido a una argentina en España. _____

5. Miguel **aprendió** a tocar la guitarra hace muchos años. Hoy ha tocado muy bien en el concierto. _____

◀ **el año pasado** –
last year
este año –
this year
de niño – *as a child*
la pelota – *the ball*
conocer –
to get to know
esta mañana –
this morning
tocar – *to play*
hace muchos años –
many years ago
hoy – *today*

*The **Indefinido***

3

The forms of the **indefinido** for regular verbs are as follows:
verbs ending in **-ar**:
canté, cantaste, cantó, cantamos, cantasteis, cantaron
verbs ending in **-er** or **-ir**:
comí, comiste, comió, comimos, comisteis, comieron

Ser and **ir** are irregular verbs: in the **indefinido** both of these verbs have identical forms (but the context will make the meaning clear): **fui, fuiste, fue, fuimos, fuisteis, fueron**

Now it's your turn! Write in the spaces the missing verb forms in the **indefinido**.

Valentina asks her friend Miguel these questions:

1. ¿Cuándo _____ por última vez a Guatemala? (viajar)

2. ¿Cuándo _____ por última vez un libro? (leer)

3. ¿Cuándo _____ por última vez un e-mail? (escribir)

4. ¿Cuándo _____ por última vez al cine? (ir)

4 TR.36

Read the dialogue. You can also listen to it on the CD.

Valentina: ¡Oye Miguel!, ¿por qué decidiste venir a estudiar a España?
Miguel: Siempre me ha atraido mucho la vida en Europa.
Valentina: Vale, pero ¿por qué a España?
Miguel: Es muy difícil estudiar en otro idioma. Y en Europa sólo se habla español aquí.
Sabes, ya soy un poco mayor y no quiero terminar mis estudios muy tarde.
Valentina: Y, ¿por qué no empezaste a estudiar antes?
Miguel: Antes trabajé.
Valentina: ¿En qué trabajaste?
Miguel: He hecho de todo. Trabajé de camarero, de cartero y de albañil. En este último trabajo decidí empezar a estudiar.
Y con el dinero ahorrado me matriculé aquí y puedo pagar mi piso.
Valentina: Y después, ¿no vas a tener problemas para trabajar como abogado en Argentina con un título español?

Miguel: Deseo dedicarme a casos comerciales internacionales. Voy a tener un título español, pero voy a seguir siendo argentino.

Valentina: ¿Casos entre empresas?

Miguel: Por ejemplo. Y tú, ¿has pensado qué vas a hacer después?

Valentina: Todavía no lo he pensado en serio.

5

Read the information about Valentina, Alicia, and Miguel. Look at the index cards and decide which sentence goes with which illustration. You can also listen to the sentences on the CD.

¡Bueno saber!

The **indefinido** is used to express actions or experiences that the speaker considers ended. Thus, the **indefinido** is often used in conjunction with expressions of time, such as **el otro día** (*the other day*), **ayer** (*yesterday*), **la semana pasada** (*last week*), **el mes pasado** (*last month*), **el año pasado** (*last year*), **en 1970** (*in 1970*).

a) Nací en Madrid en 1977. Estudié Medicina en la Universidad Complutense de Madrid.

b) Nací en Zaragoza en 1978. Ahora estudio Derecho en Madrid.

c) Nací en Buenos Aires en 1976. Viví en Córdoba hasta el año pasado y trabajé cuatro años.

6

Tener *(to have)* and **estar** *(to be)* are irregular in the **indefinido**. Both of them have very similar forms.

The **indefinido** of **tener** and **estar**:

Tener: <u>tuv</u>-e, <u>tuv</u>-iste, <u>tuv</u>-o, <u>tuv</u>-imos, <u>tuv</u>-isteis, <u>tuv</u>-ieron
Estar: <u>estuv</u>-e, <u>estuv</u>-iste, <u>estuv</u>-o, <u>estuv</u>-imos, <u>estuv</u>-isteis, <u>estuv</u>-ieron

Write the missing verb in the blanks.

1. Yo _____ una furgoneta Volkswagen.

2. Ellos _____ en América por primera vez en 1996.

3. Nosotros _____ muchas dificultades para comprender a los cubanos.

4. Él _____ un periodo en España.

5. Nosotros _____ mucha suerte en conseguir entradas.

6. Yo _____ pensando en ti.

7

Ser *(to be)* and **ir** (to go) have the same forms in the **indefinido**:
        fui, fuiste, fue, fuimos, fuisteis, fueron

Read the sentences and decide to which of the illustrated situations they correspond.

☐ a) Yo fui a Mallorca el año pasado.

☐ b) Tú fuiste de joven futbolista.

☐ c) Nosotros fuimos de compras ayer al supermercado.

☐ d) Ellas fueron muy simpáticas con los clientes.

8

Verbs with an irregular stem (the same endings are used with all of them):

querer: quise, quisiste, quiso, quisimos, quisisteis, quisieron
poner: puse, pusiste, puso, pusimos, pusisteis, pusieron
decir: dije, dijiste, dijo, dijimos, dijisteis, dijeron
hacer: hice, hiciste, hizo, hicimos, hicisteis, hicieron

> **querer** – *to want*
> **poner** – *to put, place*
> **decir** – *to say*
> **hacer** – *to do, make*

With verbs ending in **-ir** that experience a vowel change in the present tense (for example, **pedir** ▸ **(yo) pido**, **divertirse** ▸ **(yo) me divierto**), the stem vowel always changes from **e** to **i** in the **indefinido**, but only in the third persons singular and plural: **pidió, pidieron**

The spelling of some verbs changes in the **indefinido** so that the pronunciation remains the same. Thus, a **c**, **z**, or **g** at the end of the word stem and before the **e** of the first person singular changes to **qu**, **c** or **gu: buscar** *(to look for)* ▸ **busqué**

Complete the sentences with the correct verb forms.

1. Yo _____ ir a Barcelona el año pasado. (querer)

2. Él _____ los deberes en casa. (hacer)

3. Ellos _____ la verdad. (decir)

4. Nosotros _____ una tortilla de patatas para la fiesta. (hacer)

5. ¿_____ tú los cuadros en la pared? (poner)

6. Mis padres _____ ir de vacaciones con nosotros. (querer)

9

Read the sentences, choose the correct tense, and underline it.

1. Yo *nací / he nacido / nace* en 1968.
2. Ellos *estudian / han estudiado / estudiaron* en la universidad entre 1986 y 1992.
3. Siempre *nos ha gustado / nos gustó / nos gusta* mucho el chocolate sin leche.
4. Nunca *estuvimos / hemos estado / estamos* en Australia.
5. Este mes *estudié / estudio / he estudiado* mucho pero he estudiado poco español.
6. Me *casé / he casado / caso* en abril del año 2000.
7. Lo *escribo / escribí / he escrito* esta mañana.

*The **Indefinido***

10 ✏️

These syllables of some verbs in the **indefinido** are scrambled up. Put the syllables into the correct sequence.

1. mos – si – qui   _____

2. teis – es – vis – tu   _____

3. sie – ron – pu   _____

4. hi – mos – ci   _____

5. cis – hi – te   _____

6. ron – fue   _____

7. je – di   _____

11 ✏️

Complete the biography with the correct verbs. Put the verbs into the blanks.

> vivimos – estudié – nací – trabajé – tuvimos – conocí – nos casamos – vamos

1. _____ en 1970 en Salamanca.

2. Entre 1990 y 1996 _____ Informática.

3. Después _____ en la empresa Osborne, S.A.

4. En 1997 _____ a mi mujer.

5. _____ en 1999.

6. _____ nuestro primer hijo el año pasado.

7. Ahora _____ en Valencia y _____ a

   comprar una casa.

12 🖉

Read the terms and try to figure out if the **indefinido** or the **pretérito perfecto** is used with these specifications of time.

> este verano – siempre – en 1995 – este año – en una ocasión –
> por última vez – ya – hoy – el año pasado – nunca – todavía no – una vez

Indefinido	Pretérito Perfecto

▶ § 15 The Perfect Tense

▶ § 16 The **Indefinido**

13 🖉

Write the appropriate conjugated first-person singular verb form in the **indefinido** or the **perfecto** in the blanks.

1. Siempre me (gustar) _____ mucho el fútbol.

2. En 1995 (estar) _____ en México.

3. Todavía no (conocer) _____ al hijo de mi amiga.

4. El año pasado (comprarse) _____ una moto.

5. Este año (ir) _____ al casino de Montecarlo.

6. La (ver) _____ por última vez hace dos años.

7. Este verano (bañarse) _____ en las playas del Caribe.

8. Una vez (ir) _____ al circo con mi abuelo.

9. Ya (ver) _____ esa película. Es muy buena.

10. Hoy (estar) _____ con él.

11. Nunca (ver) _____ un eclipse de sol.

12. En una ocasión (encontrarse) _____ un billete
    de 50 soles.

Indefinido or *Perfecto*

14 ✏️

Put the appropriate verb forms into the blanks.

> he ido – he estado – he leído – estuve – ha ganado –
> visité – he ido – he tomado – cumplió

1. _____ ese libro tres veces o más.

2. _____ una vez en América.

3. _____ ya hoy cuatro cafés.

4. Un equipo mexicano _____ esta noche al Real Madrid

    con seis goles.

5. Nunca _____ en un concierto de José Carreras.

6. Hace dos años _____ a mi abuela en Panamá.

7. Este mes _____ unas cinco veces al cine.

8. Mi hijo _____ ayer siete años.

9. Hasta ahora _____ a América en ocho ocasiones.

15 ✏️

Put the specifications of time into the appropriate blanks.

> el otro día – ayer – el año pasado – el sábado por la noche

1. Mi familia y yo estuvimos en Sevilla _____.

2. ¿No fuiste al cine _____?

3. _____ vi a Luisa paseando con sus marido.

4. _____ no cenaron en casa. Fueron al restaurante italiano.

Indefinido or *Perfecto*

1 🖊

Look at the illustrations and complete the sentences with the **Indefinido** or the **pretérito perfecto** of **estar**, **ver**, **hablar**, and **escuchar**.

1. Valentina _____ en Ecuador de vacaciones hace dos años.

2. Ella _____ la película esta noche.

3. Valentina y Miguel _____ hoy de sus vidas.

4. Yo _____ una vez el concierto de Año Nuevo de Washington.

2 🖊

Write the missing terms in the blanks.

1. ¿Cuál es la primera persona del singular del indefinido de **trabajar**?

_____

2. ¿Cuál es la tercera persona del plural del indefinido de **comer**?

_____

3. ¿Cuál es la segunda persona del singular del indefinido de **vivir**?

_____

4. ¿Cuál es la primera persona del plural del indefinido de **estudiar**?

_____

5. ¿Cuál es la segunda persona del plural del indefinido de **correr**?

_____

6. ¿Cuál es la tercera persona del singular del indefinido de **escribir**?

_____

*The **Indefinido***

3

Read the questions and check off the correct answer. You can also listen to the questions on the CD.

1. ¿Qué hicieron ayer?
   - ☐ a. No hicieron nada especial.
   - ☐ b. Ella estuvo descansando.
   - ☐ c. Bailé toda la noche.

2. Qué cara de cansados tenéis. ¿Dónde fuisteis el sábado por la noche?
   - ☐ a. Fuimos a una discoteca muy moderna.
   - ☐ b. Fui al mercado a comprar fruta y verduras frescas.
   - ☐ c. Fue a Barcelona.

3. Esta sopa está muy picante, ¿qué pusieron en la comida?
   - ☐ a. Ponemos los libros en la estantería.
   - ☐ b. Puse el cenicero encima de la mesa.
   - ☐ c. Pusimos un poquito de chile.

4. ¿A quién dices que quisiste tanto?
   - ☐ a. Quise muchísimo a mis abuelos.
   - ☐ b. Quiero mucho a mi familia.
   - ☐ c. Quisimos entrar, pero no pudimos.

5. No sabes guardar un secreto, ¿a cuántas personas más les dijistes eso?
   - ☐ a. No digo nada.
   - ☐ b. A nadie más. Sólo se lo dije a ella.
   - ☐ c. Ha dicho que no.

6. ¿Qué estuvo haciendo durante sus vacaciones?
   - ☐ a. Estuvo durmiendo todo el día.
   - ☐ b. El mar es genial. Me gustaron mucho las vacaciones allí.
   - ☐ c. No fui de vacaciones con ella.

4

Put the verb forms in the **indefinido** into the blanks.

1. Valentina y Miguel _____ de sus pasados. (hablar)

2. Valentina _____ muchas cosas a Miguel. (preguntar)

3. Miguel _____ a una chica española en Argentina. (conocer)

4. La novia de Miguel _____ en Perú. (nacer)

1 TR.33

Read the sentences and match them up with the illustrations. You can also listen to the sentences on the CD.

| | a. Cuando era pequeña dormía muchas horas. |

| | b. De niño jugaba todos los domingos al fútbol con mis amigos. |

| | c. En Zaragoza no me gustaba ir al colegio. |

| | d. Cuando era pequeña iba mucho a la montaña. |

| | e. De pequeño nunca quería irme a dormir. |

| | f. Hace veinte años tenía una muñeca de trapo. |

> **pequeño/a** – *small*
> **de niño** – *as a child*
> **todos los domingos**
> – *every Sunday*
> **de pequeño/a** –
> *when I was little*
> **hace** – *ago*
> **la muñeca de trapo**
> – *the rag doll*
> **la hora** – *the hour*
> **el colegio** – *school*

2 TR.40

Read what happened to **Cenicienta** (*Cinderella*) in the fairy tale, and match up the sentences with the translations. You can also listen to the sentences on the CD.

1. Cenicienta viajaba en una carroza con forma de calabaza.

2. Cenicienta llevaba unos zapatos brillantes.

3. Cenicienta bailaba con el príncipe.

4. A las doce se fue muy deprisa.

5. Por el camino perdió su zapato.

a. *Cinderella danced with the prince.*

b. *Cinderella rode in a coach shaped like a pumpkin.*

c. *En route she lost a shoe.*

d. *Cinderella wore shiny shoes.*

e. *She left very quickly at midnight.*

Customary Actions in Past Time

3

Read the dialogue in which Valentina tells what she liked to do when she was a child. Mark the verbs that appear in a new past-tense form. Can you deduce from the dialogue how to construct the first person plural of the new past tense (the imperfect) for the verb **vivir**? You can also listen to the dialogue.

Miguel:	¿Qué echas de menos de tu infancia?
Valentina:	Echo de menos el grupo de montaña. Yo tuve una infancia muy aventurera. Pertenecía a un grupo de montaña y todas las semanas nos reuníamos y hacíamos actividades juntos. Vivíamos grandes aventuras y utilizábamos mucho la imaginación.
Miguel:	¿Hacían también escalada?
Valentina:	Un poco también. Aunque lo principal era salir al campo, caminar por la montaña y divertirse en grupo.
Miguel:	¿Y corrían peligro?
Valentina:	No, los responsables tenían mucho cuidado. Aunque una vez sí que pasé miedo y fue muy peligroso.
Miguel:	¿Qué les pasó?
Valentina:	Fuimos a escalar. Ese día estaba nublado. Al cabo de dos horas empezó a llover y nosotros estábamos colgados de la montaña.
Miguel:	¿Y cómo bajaron?
Valentina:	Nos bajó el equipo de rescate en montaña.
Miguel:	Y ahora, ¿vas a la montaña?
Valentina:	Sí claro, me sigue gustando muchísimo, pero ya no voy con el grupo de montaña sino con buenos amigos o con mi familia.

First person plural of the verb **vivir** in the imperfect: _____

la infancia – *the childhood*
el grupo de montaña – *mountain-climbing club*
reunirse – *to get together*
caminar – *to hike*
correr peligro – *to be in danger*
el/la responsable – *the people in charge*
tener cuidado – *to be careful*
el equipo de rescate – *the rescue team*

¡Bueno saber!

Imperfect:
First person plural:
Verbs ending in **-ar** construct the imperfect with the ending **-ábamos: trabajar – trabajábamos; hablar – hablábamos.** Verbs ending in **-er** and **-ir** construct the imperfect using the ending **-íamos: beber – bebíamos, vivir – vivíamos**

4

The imperfect tense (**imperfecto**) is one more past-tense form. All verbs have regular forms in the imperfect, except for **ser** (*to be*), **ir** (*to go*), and **ver** (*to see*).

> § 17 The Imperfect / Form

The imperfect of verbs that end in **-er** and **-ir** is the same:
él bebía, él vivía

Now it's your turn! Write the imperfect-tense forms in the blanks.

1. Nosotros _____ muchas actividades juntos. (hacer)

2. El grupo _____ con imaginación. (trabajar)

3. Nosotros lo _____ muy bien con nuestras aventuras. (pasar)

5

The imperfect is used to describe conditions, repeated actions, and customs in past time.

> **Cuando era pequeño desayunaba leche con cacao.**
> *(When I was a child I used to drink milk with cocoa.)*

Read the questions and answers concerning Miguel's habits when he was a student, and match the answers with the appropriate questions. You can also listen to the questions on the CD.

1. ¿Dónde vivías?

2. ¿Cocinabas mucho en el piso?

3. ¿Qué hacías los fines de semana?

4. ¿Practicabas algún deporte?

a. Cocinaba espaguetis con salsa boloñesa.

b. Salía por la noche.

c. Vivía en un apartamento de estudiantes.

d. Jugaba al baloncesto.

¡Bueno saber!

The imperfect is often used with such specifications as **antes** (*formerly*), **siempre** (*always*), **todos los días** (*every day*), **mientras** (*during, while*), etc. The **indefinido** with which new occurrences are expressed, is often used with specifications such as **entonces** (*then*), **de repente** (*suddenly*), **de pronto** (*all of a sudden*), **enseguida** (*immediately*), **un día** (*one day*), etc.

6

The imperfect is also used for describing situations in past time that consti-
tute the background for a new occurrence, or another important event:

> Caperucita **iba** por el bosque. De repente **encontró** al lobo.
> *(Little Red Riding Hood was going through the woods. Suddenly
> she met the wolf.)*

The following questions help with the correct usage of the verb tenses:

> What was going on? ▸ Imperfect (**Hacía** calor. *It was hot.*)
> What new event occurred? ▸ Indefinido (De repente **encontró** al lobo.
> *Suddenly she met the wolf.)*

Now it's your turn! Choose the correct verb form.

1. Caperucita *paseaba / pasea / paseó* por el bosque y
   de repente vió al lobo.
2. Colón *viajó / viajaba / viaja* a las Indias y descubrió América.
3. Todos los días *vi / veo / veía* a Pepe pero el lunes no lo vi.
4. Mientras *trabajaba / trabajó / trabaja* en el despacho era
   muy puntual.

7

These sentences come from the dialogue in this lesson between Valentina
and Miguel. Put the appropriate verbs into the spaces. Pay attention to
the tenses: **indefinido** or **imperfecto**?

> fuimos – tenía – pasaba – tuve – pasó – escalábamos –
> iba – hacíais – pasé – nos reuníamos – tenían

1. Echo de menos las vivencias que _____ con el grupo.

2. _____ una infancia muy aventurera. _____ mucho
   a la montaña.

3. Todas las semanas _____ y hacíamos actividades juntos.

4. Genial, ¿_____ también escalada?

5. Los responsables eran muy responsables y _____ mucho cuidado.

6. Nunca _____ miedo, pero una vez _____ miedo.

7. Una vez _____ a escalar. Pero normalmente no _____.

8. Afortunadamente no nos _____ nada.

8

Nearly all forms of the imperfect are regular, with the exception of the following:

> **ser** *(to be)*: **era, eras, era, éramos, erais, eran**
> **ir** *(to go)*: **iba, ibas, iba, íbamos, ibais, iban**
> **ver** *(to see)*: **veía, veías, veía, veíamos, veíais, veían**

The imperfect of **hay** is **había**.

Antes las casas **eran** pequeñas. *(In the past, houses were small.)*
La gente **iba** al trabajo a pie. *(People used to walk to work.)*
Yo casi no **veía** la televisión. *(I hardly ever watched television.)*

Now it's your turn! Choose the correct answer.

1. El profesor *era / éramos / erais* muy inteligente.
2. Las chicas *ibas / iban / iba* en metro a la escuela.
3. Vosotros no *veíamos / veían / veíais* las caras de sorpresa.

9

Think of the story of **Caperucita Roja** (*Little Red Riding Hood*) and look at the illustration. Decide if the statements are **C** (**correctas**—*true*) or **F** (**falsas**—*false*).

1. Caperucita era una niña muy buena. ☐

2. Su mamá era amiga del lobo. ☐

3. Iba por el bosque con una cesta. ☐

4. Se encontró con un oso. ☐

5. Habló con el lobo. ☐

6. La abuelita estaba enferma. ☐

7. El lobo era muy bueno. ☐

8. La caperuza de caperucita era de color azul. ☐

*The **Imperfecto***

10 ✎

Write the verb in the imperfect tense in the blanks. The infinitive of the verb to be used is given at the end of each sentence.

1. ¿Qué _____ tú de pequeña en la montaña? (hacer)

2. Yo _____ excursiones. (hacer)

3. Me _____ mucho la naturaleza y caminar por el campo. (gustar)

4. Lo mejor era cuando _____ en tienda de campaña.

   ¡Qué aventura! (dormir)

5. No necesitaba muchas cosas porque las _____ en una

   mochila. (llevar)

6. _____ el día a día con entusiasmo y fantasía. (vivir)

7. Mi estómago se quejaba porque _____ muchas sopas

   de sobre y comida de lata. (comer)

11 ✎

Imperfecto	
estaba	estábamos
estabas	estabais
estaba	estaban

Indefinido	
estuve	estuvimos
estuviste	estuvisteis
estuvo	estuvieron

Now practice the past-tense forms of the verb **estar** (*to be*). Write them in the blanks.

1. Valentina _____ el año pasado de vacaciones en Puerto Rico.

2. Luis y Alicia _____ aquí cuando Valentina estaba de vacaciones.

3. Los padres de Valentina _____ en 1992 en la Expo de Sevilla.

4. Yo no _____ en su cumpleaños.

5. ¿_____ tú en casa el lunes por la tarde?

6. Seguro que ustedes dos _____ pensando en ir al cine.

7. Después de jugar al tenis Luis y yo _____ cansados.

8. Yo _____ en casa y entonces llamó por teléfono.

9. Mi mujer y yo _____ cenando con ellos hace dos meses.

Imperfecto or *Indefinido*

12

Read the sentences from various fairy tales and decide if the verb forms are in the imperfect or the indefinido. You can also listen to the sentences on the CD.

1. Cenicienta **bailaba** con el príncipe. _____

2. Cenicienta **perdió** un zapato. _____

3. Hansel y Gretel **eran** hermanos. _____

4. La casita que **encontraron** Hansel y Gretel **era** de chocolate.

_____   _____

5. Caperucita Roja **iba** a ver a su abuelita. _____

6. Caperucita **se encontró** con el lobo. _____

7. Blancanieves **vivía** con los siete enanitos. _____

8. Blancanieves **comió** una manzana. _____

13

Match up the verbs with the sentences.

> propuso – era – queríamos – estábamos – íbamos

(1) _____ tardísimo, todos (2) _____ muy cansados

y (3) _____ irnos a casa. (4) _____ a tomar un taxi,

cuando Ana, de repente, (5) _____ ir a desayunar chocolate

con churros.

Imperfecto or *Indefinido*

14 🖊

Imperfecto or **indefinido**? Choose the correct answer.

1. Cuando *era / fui* pequeña siempre *iba / fui* al circo.
2. Mientras *estudiaba / estudié* Derecho Comercial *leía / leí* tu artículo.
3. Una vez *iba / fui* al Museo del Prado aunque no me *gustaban / gustaron* nada los museos.
4. Durante el tiempo en el que *vivía / viví* con mis padres nunca *hacía / hice* nada en casa.
5. Cada día *veía / vi* a los amigos de Juan.
6. Cuando *paseaba / paseé* por la calle me *encontraba / encontré* un billete de cien euros.
7. En el metro me *robaban / robaron* el bolso pero no *llevaba / llevé* nada de valor.
8. Siempre *llegaba / llegué* a las ocho de la tarde.

15 🖊

Imperfecto or **indefinido**? Write the correct form in the blanks.

1. ¿Tú no (dar) _____ antes un paseo todos los días?
2. (nosotros, estar) _____ cenando tranquilamente, cuando nos lo (ellos, decir) _____ .
3. ¿(vosotros, ir) _____ al cine ayer por la noche?
4. Cuando (yo, ser) _____ pequeña me (encantar) _____ ir a la playa.
5. El año pasado (ellos, viajar) _____ a Cuba.
6. (hacer) _____ tanto frío que (nosotros, decidir) _____ volver a casa.
7. El otro día (yo, ver) _____ a María hablando con Luisa.
8. Él antes (almorzar) _____ en la cantina de la empresa.

Imperfecto or *Indefinido*

1 ✐

Read the sentences. Choose the correct verb.

1. Caperucita *hablaba / hablabas / hablamos* con el lobo.

2. Blancanieves *vivían / vivíamos / vivía* con los siete enanitos del bosque.

3. Cenicienta *bailabas / bailaba / bailabais* con el príncipe.

4. Hansel y Gretel *comían / comía / comías* mucho chocolate.

5. La bella durmiente *dormían / dormíamos / dormía* mucho.

6. Los patitos *seguían / seguía / seguíais* a su mamá.

7. El flautista de Hamelin *tocaban / tocaba / tocabais* la flauta.

2 ✐

Write the appropriate verb form in the blanks.

1. First person singular imperfecto of **ir:** _____

2. First person plural imperfecto of **comer:** _____

3. First person singular indefinido of **ser:** _____

4. Second person plural imperfecto of **estar:** _____

5. First person singular indefinido of **estar:** _____

6. First person singular indefinido of **llamar:** _____

7. Third person plural imperfecto of **escribir:** _____

8. First person singular indefinido of **leer:** _____

9. Second person singular imperfecto of **leer:** _____

10. Third person plural imperfecto of **poner:** _____

The Imperfecto

3 🖉

Look at the illustrations and write the appropriate verb in the imperfect tense in the blanks.

1. Ella _____ inglés en el colegio.

2. Nosotros _____ grafitis en las paredes.

3. Ustedes _____ en América en unas camas muy grandes.

4. Tú _____ por el bosque en invierno.

4 📄

Play dominoes with verbs. The **indefinido** must find the corresponding **imperfecto** that is constructed using the same personal pronoun.

1. jugabais / esperó	2. vivíais / toqué	3. estábamos / corriste
4. trabajasteis / escribía	5. esperaba / jugó	6. estaba / fuimos
7. íbamos / trabajabais	8. iba / estuvimos	9. leyeron / fui
10. corrías / vivisteis	11. comía / estuve	12. tocaba / limpiamos
13. jugaba / comí	14. escribí / leían	15. limpiábamos / jugasteis

1

Read the sentences that describe how to prepare a **gazpacho**. The verbs in bold type are in a new verb form. You can also listen to the sentences on the CD.

el pepino – *the cucumber*	
en trozos – *into slices*	
el pimiento – *the pepper*	
el diente de ajo – *the clove of garlic*	
la miga de pan – *breadcrumbs*	
el aceite – *the oil*	
el vinagre – *the vinegar*	
cortar – *to cut*	
añadir – *to add*	
pelar – *to peel*	
echar – *to put in*	
preparar – *to prepare*	
condimentar – *to season*	
mezclar – *to mix*	
comer – *to eat*	

1. **Prepare** una sopa fría: gazpacho.

2. **Pele** los tomates y los pepinos.

3. **Corte** los tomates y los pepinos en trozos.

4. **Condimente** el gazpacho con un poco de pimiento verde y un diente de ajo.

5. **Añada** un poco de miga de pan.

6. **Eche** sal, aceite y vinagre.

7. **Mezcle** todos los ingredientes.

8. **Añada** agua.

9. **Coma** el gazpacho muy frío.

The Imperative

2 TR 45

Read the sentences and try to understand the form of the verbs. Match the sentences with the appropriate illustrations. You can also listen to the sentences on the CD.

seguir – *to follow*
el consejo – *the advice*
la verdura – *vegetables*
la fruta – *fruit*
dejar de – *to stop*
el deporte – *the sport*
poco/a – *little*
pasear – *to take a walk*

a. Para mantenerte joven **sigue** estos consejos.
b. **Come** verduras y frutas.
c. **Bebe** mucha agua.
d. **Deja** de fumar.
e. **Duerme** mucho.
f. **Haz** deporte.
g. **Bebe** poco café.
h. **Pasea** por el campo.

3 TR 46

Alicia and Luis are eating in a restaurant and talking about what they just ate. Read the conversation. You can also listen to the conversation on the CD.

el pollo al ajillo – *chicken in garlic sauce*
el secreto – *the secret*
cocinar – *to cook*
freír – *to fry*
el camarero – *the waiter*
la receta – *the recipe*

Alicia: La comida estaba buenísima. ¿Cómo se hace el pollo al ajillo?
Luis: El secreto está en echarle un buen vino.
Alicia: ¿Tú sabes cocinar esto?
Luis: Sí, es muy fácil. Primero fríe el pollo con aceite de oliva. Después añade dientes de ajo enteros y cúbrelo todo con un buen vino y cuécelo durante una hora. Eso es todo.
Alicia: No puede ser tan fácil. Le voy a preguntar al camarero... Camarero por favor, ¿nos puede dar la receta del pollo al ajillo?
Camarero: Un momento, le voy a preguntar al cocinero.

Camarero: Tiene que freír el pollo. Después añada vino y cuézalo lentamente con mucho ajo. Eso es todo.

Alicia: Tenías razón.

Luis: Tú piensas que sólo tú sabes cocinar, pero yo también cocino muy bien.

Alicia: Pienso así porque todavía no me has demostrado lo bien que cocinas.

Luis: El próximo fin de semana te voy a preparar una comida de categoría. ¿Tomamos café?

> **lentamente** – *slowly*
> **tener razón** –
> *to be right*
> **demostrar** – *to show*
> **el fin de semana** –
> *the weekend*

4

The imperative is not used only to give commands, but also for advice.

The forms are as follows:

	tú	usted	ustedes
cantar	canta	cante	canten
correr	corre	corra	corran
vivir	vive	viva	vivan

The forms of the **-er** and **-ir** verbs are identical.

Now it's your turn! Write the imperatives in the spaces.

1. _____ usted una bombilla de 50 vatios. (utilizar)

2. _____ usted la impresora a la computadora. (conectar)

3. Para grabar _____ usted las teclas play y rec. (pulsar)

> **¡Bueno saber!**
> The verb **tener + que**
> indicates an obligation.
> **Tienes que comer.**
> (*You have to eat.*) **Hay**
> **+ que** also indicates a
> duty: **Hay que trabajar**
> **de lunes a viernes.**
> (*It is necessary to work*
> *from Monday through*
> *Friday.*)

Imperative: Irregular Verbs

5

There are some verbs that are irregular even in the imperative. Look at them closely. Do you see the similarity in the **usted** and **ustedes** forms?

A few irregular verbs:

	tú	usted	ustedes
venir *(to come):*	ven	venga	vengan
poner *(to put, place):*	pon	ponga	pongan
tener *(to have, hold):*	ten	tenga	tengan
hacer *(to make, do):*	haz	haga	hagan
decir *(to say):*	di	diga	digan
ir *(to go):*	ve	vaya	vayan

Por favor María, pon la mesa. *(María, please set the table.)*
José María, ven ahora mismo. *(José María, come right now.)*

Now it's your turn! Put the imperatives into the appropriate spaces.

> haz – ven – vean – tenga – digan – pon

1. Por favor María, _____ la mesa.

2. José María, _____ ahora mismo.

3. _____ la verdad.

4. _____ cuidado con el paquete.

5. _____ la comida con poca sal.

6. _____ lo que están haciendo.

6

With affirmative imperatives the pronouns are <u>always</u> attached (see also infinitives and present participles): **déja<u>lo</u>**.

When indirect and direct object pronouns occur together, the indirect object pronoun precedes the direct.

Explíca-**me-lo**, por favor. (**me** = indirect object pronoun, **lo** = direct object pronoun). *Please explain it to me.*

In the third person **le** and **les** change to **se**:

Regála**se**lo a Valentina.

7

Read the sentences. In all sentences the imperatives are used in conjunction with pronouns. Can you check off the pronouns? You can also listen to the sentences on the CD.

1. ¡Lávate las manos!
2. ¡Dígame! – ¿Puedo hablar con Pedro, por favor?
3. Explícamelo, por favor.
4. Regálaselo (a Valentina).

8 👓

The pronouns—whether direct or indirect objects—are attached to the verb in the imperative (this is possible also with the present participle and the infinitive, but not with the negative imperative).

Put the missing words into the blanks.

1. ¿Qué están escribiendo esos chicos? _____ una carta a sus padres.

2. Tu trabajo está muy bien, _____ al profesor.

3. ¡Qué flores más bonitas! _____ a Alicia.

4. Para encontrarse bien hay que _____ después de hacer deporte.

   a. Regálaselas
   b. tomarlo
   c. enséñaselo
   d. Están escribiéndoles

9 👓

In Spanish there is an affirmative imperative for things that someone should do, and a negative imperative for things that someone should not do.

The forms of the negative imperative use the vowels opposite the ones in their infinitive endings. They are identical with the forms of the **present subjunctive**. In the polite forms of address (**usted, ustedes**) there is no difference between the affirmative and the negative imperative.

Careful: with the negative imperative the pronouns are not attached; they are placed directly before the imperative.

   ¡No te acuestes tarde! *(Don't go to bed late!)*

Verbs ending in -ar	
tú	no cantes
usted	no cante
ustedes	no canten

Verbs ending in -er	
tú	no corras
usted	no corra
ustedes	no corran

Verbs ending in -ir	
tú	no escribas
usted	no escriba
ustedes	no escriban

The Imperative

10 🖉

Write the imperative forms of the verbs in the blanks.

1. No _____ patatas fritas. (comer, ustedes)

2. No _____ con flash. (fotografiar, tú)

3. No _____ pantalón corto. (llevar, usted)

4. No _____ a los rezantes. (molestar, ustedes)

5. No _____ dentro de la iglesia. (fumar, tú)

6. No _____ con su perro. (entrar, usted)

11 🖉

Look at the pictures of a **tortilla de papas**—*a potato omelet*—and write the appropriate verbs in the imperative (second-person singular) in the blanks.

> batir – dar – pelar – comprar – freir

1. _____ un kilo de papas y media docena de huevos.

2. _____ las papas y córtalas en trozos.

3. _____ las papas con mucho aceite de oliva y muy caliente.

4. _____ los huevos y mézclalos con las papas.

5. Haz la tortilla por un lado y _____ la vuelta a la tortilla.

12 🖉

Construct individual sentences with the words provided.

1. verdad / la / di / .

_____

2. a / vayan / Montevideo / visitar / .

_____

3. a / la / ve / por / las / medicinas / farmacia / .

_____

13 🖉

Write the verbs in the imperative (**usted**) in the blanks. These are suggestions from a doctor to his patient for health and for avoiding a cold.

1. Si desea vivir mucho tiempo _____ sano. (comer)

2. _____ mucho para mantenerse jóven. (dormir)

3. _____ sin estrés para evitar el cansancio. (trabajar)

4. Si no quiere estar resfriado _____ un zumo de naranja. (beber)

5. _____ deporte a menudo. (practicar)

6. En las vacaciones _____ mucho. (descansar)

7. Para sentirse mejor _____ en un lugar tranquilo. (vivir)

◀ **sano/a** – *healthy*
joven – *young*
mantenerse – *to remain*
a menudo – *often*
descansar – *to rest*

14 🖉

Read the sentences and complete them. Which imperative verb is the right one? Check off the correct verb.

1. Paco, *déjalo / dejadlo / déjelo* en la mesa.

2. Señor López, por favor, *cómete / cómase / cómanse* todo.

3. Señores, *visítenle / visitadla / visítenla* por la noche.

4. María, *enséñaselo / enséñenselo / enseñadlo* en la biblioteca.

5. Por favor, *hazlo / hágalo / haz* rápido.

15 ✏

Write the desired verbs in the blanks:

1. Third person singular imperative of **venir** _____

2. Third person singular imperative of **poner** _____

3. Second person singular imperative of **hacer** _____

4. Third person plural imperative of **decir** _____

5. Third person singular imperative of **ir** _____

6. Second person singular imperative of **tener** _____

7. Third person plural imperative of **cocinar** _____

8. Third person singular imperative of **añadir** _____

9. Third person plural imperative of **correr** _____

10. Second person singular imperative of **cantar** _____

11. Third person plural imperative of **trabajar** _____

16 ✏

Put the verbs into the correct spaces.

> salgas – abras – cocines – vayas – comas – fumes – beba – digas

1. Cuando salgas, no _____ sola por la noche por la gran ciudad.

2. Si deseas tener una buena figura, no _____ muchas grasas.

3. No le _____ la puerta a nadie a partir de las diez de la noche.

4. Las carreteras están heladas, por favor, no _____ tan tarde hacia Arica.

5. No _____ en un hospital porque es una gran falta de respeto hacia los pacientes.

6. No _____ alcohol si conduce.

7. Todo lo que te he contado es un gran secreto y por eso no _____ nada a nadie.

8. No _____ con tanto aceite porque me sienta mal.

The Imperative

1 🖉

Write in the blanks the verbs in the second person singular imperative.

> jugar – comer – practicar – escribir – estudiar – llevar

1. _____ toda la sopa.

2. _____ deporte.

3. _____ los deberes.

4. _____ con tus amigos.

5. _____ los zapatos a su sitio.

6. _____ un poco de inglés.

2 🖉

Read the questions and check the correct answer.

1. ¿Se puede fumar aquí?
   - ▨ a. No fumes, está prohibido.
   - ▨ b. Baja a la calle con Marta.
   - ▨ c. No te bañes porque el agua está muy fría.

2. Hace mucho calor, ¿qué ropa me pongo?
   - ▨ a. No salgas por la noche.
   - ▨ b. Ponte el pantalón corto.
   - ▨ c. Mira por la ventana.

3. Me duele mucho la cabeza, ¿qué puedo hacer?
   - ▨ a. Piense en su jefe.
   - ▨ b. Descanse un poco más y no trabaje tanto.
   - ▨ c. Vaya a la discoteca.

4. ¿Vienen al cine?
   - ▨ a. Nuestra madre no nos deja salir. Ha dicho: "hoy quédense en casa".
   - ▨ b. Tengo una bicicleta azul.
   - ▨ c. Mañana va a hacer buen tiempo.

5. No podemos dejar al perro en casa, ¿lo llevamos con nosotros?
   - ▨ a. No vayas con los chicos mayores.
   - ▨ b. Deja la maleta en casa.
   - ▨ c. En el avión pone en un cartel: "No viaje con animales".

The Imperative

3

Which statement goes with which illustration? Choose the appropriate answer. You can also listen to the statements on the CD.

- ☐ a. Siéntense aquí.
- ☐ b. Duerman aquí.
- ☐ c. Coman aquí.

- ☐ a. Beban un refresco.
- ☐ b. Pónganlas en marcha.
- ☐ c. Canten una canción.

- ☐ a. Hagan los ejercicios de redacción.
- ☐ b. Hablen por teléfono.
- ☐ c. Tengan cuidado por la carretera.

- ☐ a. Duerman en este hotel.
- ☐ b. Cocinen un pastel.
- ☐ c. Pinten la pared.

- ☐ a. Viajen en barco.
- ☐ b. Vayan en este autobús.
- ☐ c. Conduzcan un taxi.

- ☐ a. Hagan muchos ejercicios.
- ☐ b. Duerman un poco.
- ☐ c. Coman mucho.

1

Read the sentences. Pay close attention to the prepositions **por** and **para**. Match the sentences with the illustrations. You can also listen to the sentences on the CD.

a. Este paquete es para mí.
b. Ellos no llamaron por no tener tiempo.
c. El avión para Cuba sale a las 10 de la mañana.
d. Caminamos por las playas de Varadero.
e. Esto no es problema para el director de la película.
f. ¿Qué te gusta tomar para desayunar?
g. ¿Cuál es la solución para el problema?
h. Por la noche no tomo nunca café.
i. El tiempo libre es muy importante para el desarrollo personal.
j. No tengo tiempo para pasar por su casa.

*Uses of **por** and **para***

2

¡Bueno saber!

Here are a few more expressions you should be aware of that use **por**: **por cierto** (*certainly*), **por fin** (*finally*), **por favor** (*please*), **gracias por** (*thanks for*)
And some that use **para**: **apto para** (*suited to*), **útil para** (*useful for*).

Para is used
- to describe a destination
- to express an opinion
- to set a time limit

Por is used
- to specify a cause
- to describe a route
- to describe an imprecise point in time
- to refer to periods during the day
- for means of transportation and communication

These examples will help you learn when **para** and **por** are used:

> **Voy para Veracruz.** (*I am going to Veracruz.*)
> **Me gusta el rojo para vestir.** (*I like to wear red.*)
> **La cena estará preparada para las diez.**
> (*The meal will be ready around ten o'clock.*)
> **Luchan por la libertad.** (*They are fighting for freedom.*)
> **Para ir al trabajo paso por el parque.**
> (*I go through the park on my way to work.*)
> **Él se levanta muy tarde por las mañanas.**
> (*He gets up very late in the morning.*)

Now it's your turn! Write **por** or **para** in the blanks.

1. Estamos _____ el centro de la ciudad.

2. Estos ejercicios son _____ el lunes.

3. Trabajan _____ vivir.

4. Todos los días hago deporte _____ la tarde.

3

Read the dialogue between Valentina, Luis, and Cecilia, Valentina's Mexican friend who is going to travel to Cuba. You can also listen to the dialogue on the CD.

la academia de cine ▶
– *the film academy*
la beca – *the scholarship*
realizar – *to make, direct*

Luis: Cecilia, ¿por qué has elegido Cuba para estudiar?

Cecilia: En Cuba hay una academia de cine muy buena. Y, además, me han concedido una beca para realizar una película allí.

Valentina: ¡Ah! Por eso te vas a Cuba. ¿Ya sabes sobre qué tema la vas a hacer?

*The Three Separate Forms of **se***

Cecilia: Tengo una idea: me interesa mucho la situación política de Cuba y quiero investigar a fondo cuáles son las perspectivas de futuro para el pueblo cubano.

Valentina: ¡A ver si te haces famosa!

Cecilia: Más que la fama, lo que me interesa es poder transmitir la realidad. Se habla mucho sobre Fidel Castro, pero lleva muchos años en el poder y quiero rodar el porqué.

Luis: Hace poco vi un documental en la televisión del turismo y de su influencia en la economía cubana. Fue muy interesante.

Cecilia: Sí, yo también lo vi.

Valentina: Es fascinante el poder de los medios de comunicación. Aunque, ¿es verdad todo lo que nos cuentan?

el pueblo – *the people*
famoso/a – *famous*
la fama – *fame*
la realidad – *reality*
el poder – *power*
la influencia – *influence*
la economía – *the economy*

In Spanish grammar there are three different uses for **se**:

1. **Se** used as a reflexive pronoun:
   Él se lava los dientes. *(He brushes his teeth.)*
2. **Se** as an indirect object pronoun when in combination with a direct object pronoun:
   Se lo digo. *(I say it to him.)*
3. **Se** as an impersonal form, for sentences with an unspecified subject:
   Se dice que el sol es malo para la piel.
   (It is said that the sun is bad for the skin.)

Now it's your turn! Match up the forms of **se** with the sentences. You can also listen to the sentences on the CD.

¡Bueno saber!
There is a phonetic reason for using **se** as an indirect object pronoun, because **lo** would immediately follow **le**, and that would not sound good. There is also a **sé** with an accent: the first person singular of the verb **saber. Yo sé.** *(I know.)*

Se impersonal form – **Se** indirect object pronoun – **Se** reflexive pronoun

1. Juan **se** lo contó todo a su madre. _____

2. **Se** comenta por la ciudad la subida de los impuestos. _____

3. **Se** lava todas las mañanas con agua y jabón. _____

Se—*Direct and Indirect Object Pronouns*

5 🖉

The word **se** is contained in all of the following sentences, but it has different meanings. Read the sentences all the way through and figure out what the word **se** means.

Example:
Ella **se** lava los dientes. Reflexive pronoun (= *herself*)

1. ¿Le compraste los billetes de avión? Sí, **se** los compré por internet.

_____

2. En Europa **se** habla mucho del turismo en Cuba. _____

3. **Se** afeita con maquinilla eléctrica. _____

4. Ella **se** sentó a mi lado a ver la película. _____

5. En el mundo del cine **se** necesita mucho capital. _____

6 👓

¡Bueno saber!

Remember that the indirect object pronouns **le / les** change to **se** when they are used with a direct object pronoun in the third person: **No se lo enseñes todavía.**

Pronouns agree in gender and number with the word they stand for, and always come immediately before the verb. When a direct and an indirect object occur together, the indirect comes before the direct.

Si no lo sabes, te lo explico yo.
(*If you don't know it, I'll explain it to you*)

The indirect object pronouns **le / les** change to **se** when followed by the direct object pronouns **lo / la / los / las**:

Se lo he explicado yo.

With an affirmative imperative and an infinitive the pronouns are attached to the verb.

With the reflexive verbs in the second person plural the **-d** is left out **(Comed + os ▶ comeos)**, as is the **-s** of the first person plural **(sentemos + nos ▶ sentémonos)**.

Both possibilities exist with the present participle.

7 🖉

Put the appropriate expressions into the blanks.

1. _____ a Javier.

2. Hay que _____ para Javier.

3. Está _____ a Javier.

4. Se _____ a Javier.

a. déjaselo
b. dejándoselo
c. lo está dejando
d. dejarlo

8

Porque is a conjunction, which joins words or sentences together.

> **No voy porque no me han invitado.**
>
> *(I'm not going because I wasn't invited.)*

El porqué is a noun and is generally used with an article.

> **No nos dijo el porqué.**
>
> *(He didn't tell us the reason.)*

Por qué is a question word used in asking about the reason or the cause for something.

> **¿Por qué no me llamas?** *(Why don't you call me?)*

Now put the appropriate expression into the blanks.

1. ¿_____ no vas al cine con tus amigos?

2. El _____ de su decisión todavía no lo sé.

3. No como _____ no tengo hambre.

a. porque
b. por qué
c. porqué

9

Write the correct preposition (**por** or **para**) in the blanks.

1. Estudio español _____ trabajar en Santo Domingo.

2. Estuve con Sofía _____ Navidad.

3. Va a la oficina de correos _____ la calle Mayor.

4. El avión _____ Haití sale a las 17 horas.

5. Quiero ir a la inauguración de la exposición _____ mi amiga.

6. Disculpe, ¿_____ ir al lavabo?

7. Ha venido María y ha preguntado _____ vosotros.

8. Hizo estas pastas _____ su cumpleaños, _____ comerlas con

   el café.

Direct and Indirect Object Pronouns

10 🖉

Look at the illustrations. Which of the sentences contains the specified pronouns?

| 1 *Se* Indirect Object Pronoun | 2 *Se* Impersonal Form | 3 *Se* Reflexive Pronoun | 4 *Le* Indirect Object Pronoun | 5 *Lo* Direct Object Pronoun |

a. Le ha dicho toda la verdad a su madre.

b. Se habla sobre Fidel Castro.

c. Ellos lo leyeron durante sus vacaciones.

d. Se lo ha dicho todo.

e. Ella se ducha todos los días.

11 🖉

Break up the chains of letters into individual words by inserting spaces at the appropriate locations.

1. Nonosgustamucholacomidapicante.

   _____

2. Medijo: "hayqueponérselatodoelverano".

   _____

3. Invéntatealgoparadarlecomoexcusa.

   _____

4. Estánviéndolaenestosmomentos.

   _____

5. Díselotodo.

   _____

6. Secreetodoloquelecuentas.

   _____

7. ¿Oshabéispuestobienlaropa?

   _____

12 ✎

Complete the sentences with the impersonal form **se** and the verb provided.

1. En España (desayunar) _____ muy poco.

2. (almorzar) _____ entre la una y las tres y media.

3. (cenar) _____ entre las nueve y las diez de la noche.

4. (salir) _____ mucho los fines de semana.

5. En los bares (tomar) _____ tapas y

   (hablar) _____ mucho.

6. (tratar) _____ a la gente de tú con más frecuencia que

   en otros países.

7. En los bares (comer) _____ un jamón muy bueno.

8. En México (hablar) _____ español.

13 ✎

Choose the correct pronouns or verbs and pronouns.

   1. *Le lo / Se lo / Se le* leyó cinco veces.
   2. *Se la / La se / Se le* ha llevado de vacaciones.
   3. *Sentémos nos / Nos sentemos / Sentémonos* aquí.
   4. *Se callen / Cállense / Callados* de una vez.
   5. *Pon lo / Lo pon / Ponlo* encima de la mesa.
   6. *Déjale / Le deja / Déja le* el juguete.
   7. *Ellos se afeitan / les afeitan / afeitense* con maquinilla.
   8. *Se le prestas / Préstaselo / Préstalose* a tu hermano.

14 ✏

Complete the following minidialogues by inserting the direct and indirect object pronouns into the correct blanks.

te – los – la – se – las – nos – lo – se

1. • ¿Por qué no me dicen quién es?

   ○ No _____ _____ podemos decir todavía.

2. • ¿Quién les ha regalado estas gafas?

   ○ _____ _____ ha regalado nuestra abuela.

3. • ¿Le has dado la agenda a la secretaria?

   ○ Sí, _____ _____ he dado esta mañana.

4. • ¿Les han comprado los regalos a sus padres?

   ○ Sí, _____ _____ hemos comprado hoy.

15 ✏

Complete the following dialogues with the correct pronouns. Pay attention to the sequence of the pronouns.

1. • ¿Quién te ha regalado estas flores?

   ○ _____ _____ ha regalado un amigo.

2. • ¿Le han comprado la blusa a la abuela?

   ○ Sí, _____ _____ hemos comprado esta tarde.

3. • ¿Quién les ha regalado los bombones?

   ○ _____ _____ han regalado los tíos.

4. • ¿Le has comprado ya a tu madre el regalo?

   ○ No, todavía no _____ _____ he comprado.

1 ✏

Write **por** or **para** in the blanks.

1. Carlos va a Cuba _____ estudiar.

2. Valentina y su hermano van a Paraguay _____ Navidad.

3. _____ la tarde estudia en la academia de cine.

4. La televisión es un medio _____ informar.

5. Estudio español _____ ir a Latinoamérica.

6. _____ el momento vivo en Estados Unidos.

2 ✏

Read the sentences. Which **se** was used in the individual sentences?
Check off the correct answer.

1. Nosotros se lo contamos todo a nuestra madre.

  a. **se** impersonal form
  b. **se** indirect object pronoun
  c. **se** reflexive pronoun

2. Se dice que en Cuba la situación económica está muy mal.

  a. **se** impersonal form
  b. **se** indirect object pronoun
  c. **se** reflexive pronoun

3. Él se pone la chaqueta.

  a. **se** impersonal form
  b. **se** indirect object pronoun
  c. **se** reflexive pronoun

4. Ella se lo lleva en el bolso.

  a. **se** impersonal form
  b. **se** indirect object pronoun
  c. **se** reflexive pronoun

5. Él se va a Cuba.

  a. **se** impersonal form
  b. **se** indirect object pronoun
  c. **se** reflexive pronoun

6. Se comenta que mañana va a nevar.

  a. **se** impersonal form
  b. **se** indirect object pronoun
  c. **se** reflexive pronoun

Por qué or *porque*

3 ✎

These sentences are scrambled up. Put the individual words back into the correct sequence.

    1. mesa / la / déjaselo / de / encima / .

    _____

    2. nunca / lo / se / no / come / .

    _____

    3. leo / me / una / tarde / en / lo / .

    _____

    4. la / casa / a / acompaño / su / .

    _____

    5. en / las / la / nos / calle / encontramos / .

    _____

    6. a / trabajándolo / fondo / están / .

    _____

4 ✎

Por qué or **porque**? Put the correct variant into the appropriate spaces.

    1. No viene _____ no quiere.

    2. ¿_____ no me lo das?

    3. Tengo hambre _____ he hecho mucho deporte.

    4. Voy al cine _____ la película es muy interesante.

    5. ¿_____ has llegado tan tarde a casa?

    6. Voy con José _____ Luis no puede venir conmigo.

    7. ¿_____ no vamos de vacaciones este verano
       a Costa Rica?

    8. _____ Costa Rica está muy lejos.

*The Prepositions **a**, **de**, and **en***

1

Valentina and Cecilia are in a café in a department store. Read the sentences and pay attention to the prepositions **a** and **de**. You can also listen to the sentences on the CD.

1. El zumo **de** naranja está frío.
2. La corbata que llevo es **de** seda.
3. La chaqueta **de** piel es muy cara.
4. La torta **de** fresa es riquísima.
5. Luis va **a** llamar **a** las cinco.
6. Mañana voy **a** viajar en avión.
7. Escriben una postal **a** sus amigos.
8. Aplauden **al** pianista.

2

The prepositions **a** and **en** don't always correspond to the literal translation in English. **A** normally is used with verbs of motion; **en** is somewhat more static.

The preposition **a** is used as follows:
- Before a direct object that refers to a person:
  ¿Conoces **a** María?
- Before an indirect object:
  Da las llaves **a** María.
- To specify a direction:
  Hoy vamos **a** Guadalajara.
- To show when an action begins or ends:
  Nos vemos **a** las tres.
  La clase es de diez **a** dos.
- To clarify type or manner:
  Carne **a** la brasa.

*Use of **a** and **en***

Read the sentences and pronounce them. Consider when the preposition **a** is used. You can also listen to the sentences on the CD.

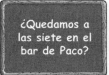

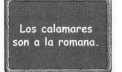

Escribe a Juan una carta.

¿Quedamos a las siete en el bar de Paco?

Los calamares son a la romana.

Quiero a mis amigos.

3

When to use the preposition **en**:

- To specify time and place:
  En Semana Santa vamos a Sevilla. (*We are going to Sevilla for Easter.*)
  Madrid está **en** España. (*Madrid is in Spain.*)
- To specify the type of transportation used:
  Voy **en** tren al trabajo. (*I take the train to work.*)
- With languages:
  El libro es **en** español. (*The book is in Spanish.*)

Put the correct expressions into the blanks.

> en México – en España – en matemáticas – en avión

1. En Navidad se come turrón _____.

2. Acapulco está en _____.

3. Vuelo _____ una vez al año.

4. Ella es muy buena _____.

Verbs with Prepositions

4

Read the dialogue involving Cecilia, Valentina, and Luis. Cecilia is going to move into Valentina's and Luis's neighborhood. You can also listen to the dialogue on the CD.

Valentina: ¿Cuándo te vas a trasladar?

Cecilia: Creo que a mediados del próximo mes. Depende de la empresa de mudanzas.

Valentina: ¿Te apetece venir a vivir a nuestro barrio?

Cecilia: Mucho, pero cuando pienso en la mudanza se me quitan las ganas. Últimamente sueño con la mudanza. En mis sueños empaco cosas, traslado cajas de un lado a otro y nunca acabo.

Valentina: ¿Por qué no dejas de trabajar unos días y te dedicas a la mudanza por completo?

Cecilia: No puedo. Tengo que cumplir con mis obligaciones y no puedo dedicarme a otra cosa en las horas de trabajo.

Valentina: Tienes que aprender a vivir un poco más y a no pensar tanto en el trabajo.

Cecilia: Es fácil decirlo, pero en mi posición no puedo permitírmelo.

Luis: Entonces, paga a alguien para que te ayude con el traslado.

Cecilia: No es cuestión de dinero. Sólo yo sé en qué lugar van las cosas que tengo.

Luis: Nosotros te podemos ayudar. ¿Verdad Valentina?

Valentina: Por supuesto.

Cecilia: Son muy amables.

> **¡Bueno saber!**
> The second person plural verb form is not used in Latin America; instead, the third person plural is used. Thus, **Son muy amables** can mean *They are very friendly* or *You* (plural) *are very friendly.*

> **trasladarse** – *to move*
> **trasladar** – *to move*
> **a mediados** – *in the middle*
> **depender de** – *to depend on*
> **la empresa de mudanzas** – *the moving company*
> **el barrio** – *the neighborhood*
> **la mudanza** – *the move*
> **el sueño** – *the dream*
> **empacar** – *to pack*
> **la caja** – *the box*
> **dejar de** – *to stop*
> **dedicarse a** – *to devote oneself to*
> **permitir** – *to allow, permit*
> **por supuesto** – *of course, naturally*

5 _✐

The sentence fragments on the left side don't match the fragments on the right. Match up the sentence fragments on the left with the appropriate ones on the right. Pay particular attention to the prepositions.

1. Los niños aprendieron	a. de dirección?
2. ¿Cuándo han empezado	b. con Argentina y Perú.
3. Ha venido a trabajar	c. a leer en la escuela.
4. Se parece	d. a Alemania.
5. El médico dice que deje	e. con ella.
6. ¿Has cambiado	f. de fumar.
7. Me acuerdo mucho	g. a su padre.
8. El otro día soñé	h. de mi estancia en Madrid.
9. Chile limita	i. a aprender español?
10. En la panadería trato	j. con mucha gente.

6

Verbs that use the preposition **a** include the following:
- Verb + **a** + infinitive:
  Los niños aprenden **a** leer. *(The children are learning to read.)*
- Verbs of motion that specify a purpose (Verb + **a**):
  Salgo **a** comprar. *(I'm going shopping.)*
- There are some verbs that take on a different meaning in combination with the preposition **a**:

Verbos + a + infinitivo:	Verbos de movimiento + a:
atreverse a – *to dare to*	**bajar a** – *to go down to*
enseñar a – *to teach, show*	**salir a** – *to go out*
negarse a – *to refuse*	**venir a** – *to come*
echarse a – *to do something all of a sudden*	**ir a** – *to go*
aprender a – *to learn to*	**subir a** – *to go up*
empezar a – *to begin to*	**llegar a** – *to arrive at*
jugar a – *to play*	
referirse a – *to refer to*	

Verbs that change meaning in combination with **a**:

dedicar – *to dedicate*
dedicarse a – *to occupy oneself with*

parecer – *to seem, appear*
parecerse a – *to look like someone*

limitar – *to border*
limitarse a – *to limit oneself to*

7

Choose the appropriate verbs for these sentences:

1. He venido a *lavarle / explicarle / dormirme* el problema.
2. Me *voy / vengo / niego* a irme.
3. Los niños aprendieron a *esquiar / hicieron / tuvieron* en las vacaciones.
4. Me *limito / escribo / hago* a leer estas líneas.

8

Verbs that use the preposition **de** include the following:

Verbs + **de** + infinitive:
Acabo de escuchar la canción. *(I have just listened to the song.)*
Verbs + **de** + noun:
Hemos cambiado de teléfono. *(We have a new phone number.)*

The preposition **de**:
- Origin
  un chico de Haití *(a youngster from Haiti)*
- Subject, contents, or composition:
  un zumo de naranja *(an orange juice)*
  una película de terror *(a horror movie)*
- Ownership or belonging:
  la casa de mis padres *(my parents' house)*

> **¡Bueno saber!**
> There are some verbs that take on a different meaning in combination with **de**.
> **Me acuerdo de mi madre todos los días.**
> *I think of my mother every day.*
> **Acordamos vernos a las seis en su casa.**
> *We agreed to meet at six o'clock at her house.*

*Verbs with **de***

Verbs + **de** + infinitive:

acabar de – *to have just done something*
no acabar de – *to not be able to
do something*
dejar de – *to stop*
no dejar de – *to not neglect to
do something*

Verbs + **de** + noun:

disponer de – *to have at one's disposal*
cambiar de – *to change something
or someone*
tratar de – *to try to*
morir de – *to die of something*

Verbs that change meaning with **de**:

acordar – *to conclude, resolve*
acordarse de – *to remember something or someone*
informar – *to inform*
informarse de – *to find out about*
olvidar – *to forget*
olvidarse de – *to forget something*

9

Read these examples. You can also listen to them on the CD.

> **Acabo de** beberme el café.
>
> La película no la **acabo de** entender.
>
> Tengo que **dejar de** salir tanto por la noche.
>
> No **dejes de** beber dos litros de agua al día.
>
> No te localicé, ¿**has cambiado de** teléfono?
>
> **Me muero de** ganas de ir a Guatemala.

10

Answer the questions and choose the correct answer. There is only one correct answer.

1. ¿Con qué países limita España?
   - ☐ a. España tiene frontera con Francia y Portugal.
   - ☐ b. España no limita con Francia.
   - ☐ c. España está en Europa.

2. Cecilia, ¡cuéntame tus sueños!
   - ☐ a. Duermo mucho porque estoy muy cansada.
   - ☐ b. Me voy a comprar el periódico.
   - ☐ c. Últimamente sueño con la mudanza.

3. ¿Por qué no le hablas? ¿Estás enfadado con él?
   - ☐ a. Soy tan feliz en mi trabajo.
   - ☐ b. Sí, estoy muy enfadado con mi amigo y por eso no le hablo.
   - ☐ c. Tengo ganas de ir a comer una pizza.

4. ¿Por qué está tu hermano siempre enfermo?
   - ☐ a. Sí que puedo quedar contigo.
   - ☐ b. Porque trabaja en un hospital y trata mucho con enfermos.
   - ☐ c. Me gusta mucho el chocolate.

11 ✎

Look at the pictures and complete the sentences with the appropriate preposition: **a**, **en**, or **de**.

1. He puesto la compra _____ la bolsa.

2. Voy _____ cenar _____ casa de mis amigos.

3. Estoy _____ casa desde las siete.

4. Queremos mucho _____ nuestros hijos.

5. El marco _____ plata está encima del armario.

◀ **la compra** – *the purchase*
la bolsa – *the bag*
el marco de plata – *the silver frame*
el armario – *the cabinet*

Verbs with Prepositions

12 TR. 56 ✎

Read the questions that Cecilia is asked and choose the appropriate verb. You can also listen to these questions on the CD.

1. ¿Qué haces?
   Estoy *empezando / enseñando / echándome* a preparar mi mudanza.

2. ¿Con quién sales a cenar esta noche?
   Salgo / Llego / Subo a cenar con Luis y Valentina.

3. ¿Se parecen Luis y Valentina?
   No, no *se parecen / se dejan / se limitan* en nada.

4. ¿Con qué sueñas?
   Sueño / Cumplo / Me atrevo con la mudanza.

5. ¿Te enfadas con Luis?
   No, no *me enfado / pienso / dejo* con Luis porque es sincero conmigo.

6. ¿Con quién hablabas?
   Acabo / Dejo / Sueño de hablar con Miguel por teléfono.

13 ✎

Write an appropriate preposition for each verb.

1. aparcamos _____
2. llegada _____
3. salida _____
4. pasamos _____
5. vemos _____
6. viajamos _____
7. circulamos _____
8. comemos _____

> a – de – en – en – por – a – en – por

1 ✏

Write the missing prepositions **a**, **de**, or **en** in the blanks.

1. ¿Has comido alguna vez pulpo _____ la gallega?

2. El anillo es _____ plata.

3. Nos vemos _____ las dos.

4. ¿Conoces _____ mi madre?

5. Luis es bueno _____ Historia.

6. Hoy viajamos de Santiago _____ Talca.

7. _____ el fondo no es mala persona.

2 ✏

These sentences are scrambled up. Put the individual words back into the correct sequence.

1. dejan / medios / dar / la / los / no / de / noticia / .

_____

2. fumar / médico / que / de / dejar / el / dice / debes / .

_____

3. ella / acaba / no / trabajo / de / de / encontrar / puesto / buen / un / .

_____

4. limitó / se / a / la / verdad / decir / testigo / el / .

_____

5. simpático / Luis / parece / .

_____

6. dedican / vecinos / carpintería / se / mis / la / a / .

_____

7. tarde / lunes / la / por / sol / el / tomar / a / calle / baja / la / a / los / .

_____

8. cambiar / todavía / piso / no / quiere / de / .

_____

A, de, en, or *con*

3 🖉

Put the correct verbs and prepositions into the blanks.

1. _____ hablar de una vez por teléfono.

2. México _____ los Estados Unidos y con otros países.

3. Me _____ mi infancia.

4. _____ vacaciones.

5. Me _____ todo.

> a. olvido de   b. limita con   c. deja de   d. acuerdo de   e. vamos de

4 🖉

Write the correct prepositions in the blanks. Choose among **a**, **de**, **en**, and **con**.

1. Sueño _____ el mar.

2. ¿Me vas a obligar _____ ir contigo?

3. El juez le obligó _____ decir la verdad.

4. Estuvo toda la noche pensando _____ él.

5. Pensaron _____ una solución.

6. He soñado _____ la película.

7. Deja _____ llorar.

8. El niño no se atreve _____ cruzar la calle solo.

1

Exercise 3
1. tardes; 2. soy; 3. yo; 4. tal; 5. tú; 6. es;
7. llamo; 8. gracias; 9. adiós; 10. luego

Exercise 7
1. el; 2. la; 3. el

Exercise 8
1. la; 2. la; 3. el; 4. la; 5. el; 6. el; 7. el; 8. el;
9. la; 10. el; 11. la; 12. la

Exercise 10
1. b; 2. c; 3. a; 4. d

Exercise 12
1. yo; 2. ella; 3. él; 4. ella; 5. tú

Exercise 13
Illustration 1 – Dialogue b;
Illustration 2 – Dialogue c;
Illustration 3 – Dialogue a

Exercise 14
1. s/d; 2. p; 3. s/d; 4. p; 5. p; 6. s/d

Exercise 15
1. sois; 2. son; 3. eres; 4. soy; 5. es; 6. somos

Exercise 16
1. c; 2. d; 3. f; 4. a; 5. e; 6. b

Test 1

Exercise 1
1. b; 2. c; 3. c; 4. a; 5. c; 6. a

Exercise 2
1. s/d; 2. s/d; 3. p; 4. p; 5. s/d; 6. p; 7. s/d;
8. p; 9. p; 10. p

Exercise 3
1. la; 2. el; 3. el; 4. la; 5. la; 6. el

Exercise 4
1. soy; 2. eres; 3. soy; es; 4. sois; 5. son;
6. somos; 7. es; 8. es; 9. somos; 10. son

2

Exercise 1
1. d; 2. e; 3. b; 4. c; 5. a

Exercise 3
¿De dónde?

Exercise 5
1. trabaja; 2. comen; 3. vive; 4. trabajo

Exercise 7
1. unos; 2. unas; 3. una; 4. un

Exercise 9
-s; -es

Exercise 11
1. Yo no soy Valentina,; 2. No somos de Chile,;
3. No trabajo en un hospital,; 4. no como carne.

Exercise 13
1. dónde; 2. de; 3. eres; 4. soy

Exercise 14
1. c; 2. d; 3. g; 4. h; 5. b; 6. f; 7. a; 8. e

Exercise 15
1. unos; 2. una; 3. unas; 4. un

Exercise 16
1. ciudades; 2. unas; 3. amigos; 4. hermanas;
5. estos; 6. teléfonos

Exercise 17
1. unas casas; 2. un coche; 3. unas lámparas;
4. unos libros; 5. un cuaderno;
6. unos ordenadores; 7. unos teléfonos;
8. una silla; 9. unas mesas; 10. un hospital

Modules 2 through 4

Test **2**

Exercise 1
1. b; **2.** a; **3.** c; **4.** a

Exercise 2
1. vivís; **2.** trabajamos; **3.** toman;
4. comprendes; **5.** trabajo; **6.** escribe

Exercise 3
1. Unos libros; **2.** Una silla; **3.** Un móvil; **4.** Unos
ordenadores; **5.** Un teléfono; **6.** Unas mesas

3

Exercise 2
1. d; **2.** c; **3.** b; **4.** e; **5.** a

Exercise 4
1. está – estoy; **2.** están – estamos

Exercise 6
1. b; **2.** d; **3.** a; **4.** c

Exercise 8
1b; 2a; 3b; 4a; 5b; 6a

Exercise 9
1. b; **2.** c; **3.** a

Exercise 10
1. pequeño; **2.** simpáticas; **3.** modernas;
4. grandes; **5.** pocos; **6.** mucha; **7.** muchas;
8. antiguos

Exercise11
1. francés; **2.** española; **3.** italianos;
4. mexicanas; **5.** alemana; **6.** belga;
7. portugués; **8.** suizas

Exercise 12
1. c; **2.** b; **3.** e; **4.** f; **5.** d; **6.** a

Exercise 13
No specific answers

Test **3**

Exercise 1
1. a; **2.** a; **3.** c; **4.** b; **5.** a; **6.** c

Exercise 2
1. es; **2.** está; **3.** es; **4.** está; **5.** es

Exercise 3
1. b; **2.** c; **3.** a; **4.** c

Exercise 4
1. muy; **2.** mucho; **3.** mucho; **4.** mucho; **5.** muy;
6. muy; **7.** mucho; **8.** muy

4

Exercise 3
1. está; **2.** es; **3.** soy – soy – estoy

Exercise 5
1. voy; **2.** va; **3.** van

Exercise 6
1. vas a; **2.** va a; **3.** van a; **4.** van a

Exercise 8
1. está; **2.** hay; **3.** está; **4.** hay

Exercise 9
1. en ; **2.** en; **3.** a; **4.** en – en

Exercise 10
1. estoy; **2.** está; **3.** está; **4.** es; **5.** es; **6.** están;
7. es; **8.** estás

Exercise 11
1. vamos a pasar; **2.** voy a hacer;
3. va a viajar; **4.** van a pasear; **5.** vais a comer;
6. voy a empezar

Exercise 12
1. está; **2.** están; **3.** son; **4.** es

Exercise 13
1. c; **2.** b; **3.** a; **4.** b; **5.** a

Test **4**

Exercise 1
1. hay; **2.** está; **3.** están; **4.** hay

Exercise 2
1. en; **2.** en; **3.** a; **4.** en

Exercise 3
1c; 2a; 3c; 4b

Exercise 4
1. a; **2.** b; **3.** c; **4.** a

5

Exercise 2
You like one thing: 1; 3; 5; 7; 9
You like several things: 2; 4; 6; 8; 10

Exercise 4
1. me gusta; **2.** nos gustan; **3.** le gusta;
4. os gustan

Exercise 5
1. e; **2.** f; **3.** b; **4.** c; **5.** a; **6.** d

Exercise 7
1. a mí; **2.** a ella; **3.** a nosotros; **4.** a ellos

Exercise 9
1. quiere, quiero; **2.** queremos; **3.** quieren;
4. quieres

Exercise 12
1. salgo; **2.** sabe; **3.** sé

Exercise 13
a. sé; **b.** traduzco; **c.** queréis; **d.** dormimos;
e. sientes; **f.** puedo; **g.** piensan; **h.** conozco;
i. cuenta

Exercise 14
1. le; **2.** me; **3.** le; **4.** nos; **5.** le; **6.** les;
7. os; **8.** te

Exercise 15
1. a; **2.** b; **3.** c; **4.** b; **5.** a; **6.** c

Exercise 16
1. piensa; **2.** sabéis; **3.** entiendo; **4.** quieres;
5. ponen; **6.** veo; **7.** vuelves; **8.** cuestan

Exercise 17
1. A mí me encanta estudiar en las vacaciones.
2. ¿Te gusta trabajar en una empresa internacional?
3. A ellos les gustan las fiestas en los pueblos.
4. A Marta y a mí nos gustan los coches
alemanes.
5. A él le interesa la política.
6. ¿A ustedes les fascina el jazz?

Test **5**

Exercise 1
1a; 2b; 3c; 4a; 5c; 6a

Exercise 2
1. le; **2.** les; **3.** te; **4.** nos

Exercise 3
1. conozco; **2.** podéis; **3.** sentís; **4.** empieza;
5. prefieres; **6.** entienden

Exercise 4
1. b; **2.** a; **3.** b

Modules 6 and 7

6

Exercise 3
1. me despierto; 2. te levantas; 3. se ducha;
4. se lava; 5. nos vestimos; 6. os desvestís;
7. se acuestan

Exercise 5
1. b; 2. e; 3. d; 4. a; 5. c

Exercise 7
1. pide; 2. consigue; 3. eliges; 4. sigue

Exercise 8
1. tiene; 2. dicen; 3. vienes

Exercise 9
1. se levanta; 2. me ducho; 3. nos despertamos;
4. se acuestan; 5. os llamáis; 6. te lavas

Exercise 10
1. dices; 2. repetís; 3. está; 4. digo; 5. repite;
6. eligen

Exercise 11
1. traduzco; 2. puedes; 3. entiendo; 4. cuestan;
5. tengo; 6. juegan

Exercise 12
1. Sí, los compro en la librería.
2. Sí, la voy a ver.
3. Sí, Gabriel lo compra.
4. Sí, las quiero.
5. Sí, los prefiero.

Exercise 13
1. se afeita; 2. me adapto; 3. se preocupan;
4. nos encontramos; 5. se atreven; 6. se llevan

Exercise 14
1. vais; 2. podeis; 3. va; 4. quieren, pueden;
5. van; 6. quieres

Exercise 15
1. A mí me gusta la televisión.
2. Te quiero ver.
3. Me lo dices.
4. A Valentina le encanta hablar.
5. A mí no me importa.
6. No puedo hacerlo.
7. Los compro en el supermercado.
8. La llamo por teléfono.

Exercise 16
1. la; 2. las; 3. los; 4. lo; 5. las

Test 6

Exercise 1
1. cuesta; 2. tienes; 3. encuentro; 4. eres;
5. preferimos; 6. sé

Exercise 2
1a; 2b; 3b; 4b

Exercise 3
1. los; 2. la; 3. lo; 4. las

Exercise 4
1. soy; 2. nos lavamos; 3. dicen; 4. juegas;
5. os acostáis; 6. haces; 7. vengo; 8. van;
9. estamos; 10. decís; 11. tengo;
12. se despierta

7

Exercise 1
1. c; 2. d; 3. b; 4. e; 5. a

Exercise 3
1. estudiando; 2. hablando por teléfono

Exercise 5
1. a; 2. c; 3. b; 4. f; 5. e; 6. d

Exercise 6
1. se ha casado; 2. ha sido; 3. ha llevado;
4. ha habido; 5. hemos comido

Exercise 7
1. abierto; 2. visto; 3. vuelto; 4. puesto

Exercise 9
1. nada; 2. ningún; 3. no; 4. nadie

Exercise 11
1. ¿Has visto a Ana? Sí, la he visto.
2. ¿Se han duchado esta mañana?
   Sí, se han duchado.
3. ¿Te lo ha dicho? No, no me lo ha dicho.

Exercise 12
1a; 2c; 3b; 4c

Exercise 13
1. me he levantado; 2. he decorado;
3. he invitado; 4. me he bañado, me he vestido;
5. ha sido; 6. me he acostado; 7. ha sido

Exercise 14
Regular:
leído, comido, bailado, vivido, querido, jugado;
Irregular:
puesto, visto, abierto, hecho, ido, vuelto

Exercise 15
1. al jugador; 2. la tarta de chocolate;
3. a nuestros amigos; 4. el concierto;
5. las rosas; 6. a las francesas

Test **7**

Exercise 1
1. está jugando; 2. están corriendo;
3. estás bailando; 4. estoy leyendo

Exercise 2
1. he vuelto; 2. hemos cantado; 3. has puesto;
4. habéis dicho; 5. ha hecho; 6. han abierto

Exercise 3
1. lo; 2. la; 3. lo; 4. le; 5. los; 6. las; 7. les

Exercise 4
1. a, d; 2. c, e; 3. b, f

Exercise 5
1. han ido; 2. hacer; 3. cantando; 4. sus;
5. somos; 6. ha abierto; 7. estudiando; 8. leer;
9. he dicho; 10. estando; 11. mis; 12. habéis ido

8

Exercise 1
1. a; 2. c; 3. d; 4. e; 5. b

Exercise 2
1. estudiar; 2. viajar; 3. jugar; 4. conocer;
5. aprender

Exercise 3
1. viajaste; 2. leíste; 3. escribiste; 4. fuiste

Exercise 5
1. b; 2. c; 3. a

Exercise 6
1. tuve; 2. estuvieron; 3. tuvimos; 4. estuvo;
5. tuvimos; 6. estuve

Exercise 7
1. b; 2. d; 3. a; 4. c

Exercise 8
1. quise; 2. hizo; 3. dijeron; 4. hicimos;
5. pusiste; 6. quisieron

Exercise 9
1. nací; 2. estudiaron; 3. nos ha gustado;
4. hemos estado; 5. he estudiado; 6. casé;
7. he escrito

Modules 8 and 9

Exercise 10
1. quisimos; 2. estuvisteis; 3. pusieron;
4. hicimos; 5. hiciste; 6. fueron; 7. dije

Exercise 11
1. nací; 2. estudié; 3. trabajé; 4. conocí;
5. nos casamos; 6. tuvimos; 7. vivimos, vamos

Exercise 12
Expressions with the indefinido:
en 1995, en una ocasión, por última vez,
el año pasado, una vez
Expressions with p. perfecto:
este verano, siempre, este año, ya, hoy, nunca,
todavía no

Exercise 13
1. ha gustado; 2. estuve; 3. he conocido;
4. me compré; 5. he ido; 6. vi; 7. me he bañado;
8. fui; 9. he visto; 10. he estado; 11. he visto;
12. me encontré

Exercise 14
1. he leído; 2. estuve; 3. he tomado;
4. ha ganado; 5. he estado; 6. visité; 7. he ido;
8. cumplió; 9. he ido

Exercise 15
1. el año pasado; 2. ayer; 3. el otro día;
4. el sábado por la noche

Test **8**

Exercise 1
1. estuvo; 2. ha visto; 3. han hablado;
4. escuché

Exercise 2
1. trabajé; 2. comieron; 3. viviste;
4. estudiamos; 5. corristeis; 6. escribió

Exercise 3
1. a; 2. a; 3. c; 4. a; 5. b; 6. a

Exercise 4
1. hablaron; 2. preguntó; 3. conoció; 4. nació

9

Exercise 1
1. d; 2. b; 3. e; 4. f; 5. a; 6. c

Exercise 2
1. b; 2. d; 3. a; 4. e; 5. c

Exercise 3
vivíamos

Exercise 4
1. hacíamos; 2. trabajaba; 3. pasábamos

Exercise 5
1. c; 2. a; 3. b; 4. d

Exercise 6
1. paseaba; 2. viajaba; 3. veía; 4. trabajaba

Exercise 7
1. tenía; 2. tuve, iba; 3. nos reuníamos;
4. hacíais; 5. tenían; 6. pasaba, pasé;
7. fuimos, escalábamos; 8. pasó

Exercise 8
1. era; 2. iban; 3. veíais

Exercise 9
1. C; 2. F; 3. C; 4. F; 5. C; 6. C; 7. F; 8. F

Exercise 10
1. hacías; 2. hacía; 3. gustaba; 4. dormía;
5. llevaba; 6. vivía; 7. comía

Exercise 11
1. estuvo; 2. estuvieron; 3. estuvieron;
4. estuve; 5. estuviste; 6. estaban;
7. estábamos; 8. estaba; 9. estuvimos

Exercise 12
1. Imperfekt; **2.** Indefinido; **3.** Imperfekt;
4. Indefinido, Imperfekt; **5.** Imperfekt;
6. Indefinido; **7.** Imperfekt; **8.** Indefinido

Exercise 13
1. era; **2.** estábamos; **3.** queríamos; **4.** íbamos;
5. propuso

Exercise 14
1. era, iba; **2.** estudiaba, leí; **3.** fui, gustaban;
4. viví, hice; **5.** veía; **6.** paseaba, encontré;
7. robaron, llevaba; **8.** llegaba

Exercise 15
1. dabas; **2.** estábamos, dijeron; **3.** fuisteis;
4. era, encantaba; **5.** viajaron;
6. hacía, decidimos; **7.** vi; **8.** almorzaba

Test **9**

Exercise 1
1. hablaba; **2.** vivía; **3.** bailaba; **4.** comían;
5. dormía; **6.** seguían; **7.** tocaba

Exercise 2
1. iba; **2.** comíamos; **3.** fui; **4.** estabais;
5. estuve; **6.** llamé; **7.** escribían; **8.** leí;
9. leías; **10.** ponían

Exercise 3
1. estudiaba; **2.** escribíamos; **3.** dormían;
4. corrías

Exercise 4
1; 5; 13; 11; 6; 7; 4; 14; 9; 8; 3; 10; 2; 12; 15

10

Exercise 2
a. 3; **b.** 7; **c.** 4; **d.** 2; **e.** 8; **f.** 6; **g.** 1; **h.** 5

Exercise 4
1. utilice; **2.** conecte; **3.** pulse

Exercise 5
1. pon; **2.** ven; **3.** digan; **4.** tenga; **5.** haz;
6. vean

Exercise 7
1. lávate; **2.** dígame; **3.** explícamelo;
4. regálaselo

Exercise 8
1. d; **2.** c; **3.** a; **4.** b

Exercise 10
1. coman; **2.** fotografíes; **3.** lleve; **4.** molesten;
5. fumes; **6.** entre

Exercise 11
1. compra; **2.** pela; **3.** fríe; **4.** bate; **5.** da

Exercise 12
1. Di la verdad.
2. Vayan a visitar Montevideo.
3. Ve a la farmacia por las medicinas.

Exercise 13
1. coma; **2.** duerma; **3.** trabaje; **4.** beba;
5. practique; **6.** descanse; **7.** viva

Exercise 14
1. déjalo; **2.** cómase; **3.** visítenla;
4. enséñaselo; **5.** hágalo

Exercise 15
1. venga; **2.** ponga; **3.** haz; **4.** digan; **5.** vaya;
6. ten; **7.** cocinen; **8.** añada; **9.** corran;
10. canta; **11.** trabajen

Exercise 16
1. vayas; **2.** comas; **3.** abras; **4.** salgas; **5.** fumes;
6. beba; **7.** digas; **8.** cocines

Test 10

Exercise 1
1. come; **2.** practica; **3.** escribe; **4.** juega;
5. lleva; **6.** estudia

Exercise 2
1. a; **2.** b; **3.** b; **4.** a; **5.** c

Exercise 3
1. a; **2.** b; **3.** c; **4.** a; **5.** b; **6.** a

11

Exercise 1
a. 3; **b.** 8; **c.** 2; **d.** 10; **e.** 1; **f.** 9; **g.** 5;
h. 6; **i.** 7; **j.** 4

Exercise 2
1. por; **2.** para; **3.** para; **4.** por

Exercise 4
1. Se indirect object pronoun; **2. Se** impersonal
form; **3. Se** reflexive pronoun

Exercise 5
1. Indirect object pronoun **le**, which changes to
   se when used in combination with **los**
2. impersonal form **one**, or passive voice
3. reflexive pronoun
4. reflexive pronoun
5. impersonal form **one**, or passive voice

Exercise 7
1. a; **2.** d; **3.** b; **4.** c

Exercise 8
1. b; **2.** c; **3.** a

Exercise 9
1. para; **2.** por; **3.** por; **4.** para; **5.** por; **6.** para;
7. por; **8.** por, para

Exercise 10
1. d.; **2.** b.; **3.** e.; **4.** a.; **5.** c.

Exercise 11
1. No nos gusta mucho la comida picante.
2. Me dijo: "hay que ponérsela todo el verano".
3. Invéntate algo para darle como excusa.
4. Están viéndola en estos momentos.
5. Díselo todo.
6. Se cree todo lo que le cuentas.
7. ¿Os habéis puesto bien la ropa?

Exercise 12
1. se desayuna; **2.** se almuerza; **3.** se cena;
4. se sale; **5.** se toman, se habla; **6.** se trata;
7. se come; **8.** se habla

Exercise 13
1. Se lo; **2.** Se la; **3.** Sentémonos; **4.** Cállense;
5. Ponlo; **6.** Déjale; **7.** se afeitan; **8.** Préstaselo

Exercise 14
1. te lo; **2.** nos las; **3.** se la; **4.** se los

Exercise 15
1. me las; **2.** se la; **3.** nos los; **4.** se lo

Test 11

Exercise 1
1. para; 2. por; 3. por; 4. para; 5. para; 6. por

Exercise 2
1. b; 2. a; 3. c; 4. b; 5. c; 6. a

Exercise 3
1. Déjaselo encima de la mesa.
2. No se lo come nunca.
3. Me lo leo en una tarde.
4. La acompaño a su casa.
5. Nos las encontramos en la calle.
6. Están trabajándolo a fondo.

Exercise 4
1. porque; 2. por qué; 3. porque; 4. porque;
5. por qué; 6. porque; 7. por qué; 8. porque

12

Exercise 3
1. en España; 2. en Alemania; 3. en avión;
4. en matemáticas

Exercise 5
1. c; 2. i; 3. d; 4. g; 5. f; 6. a; 7. h;
8. e; 9. b; 10. j

Exercise 7
1. explicarle; 2. niego; 3. esquiar; 4. limito

Exercise 10
1. a; 2. c; 3. b; 4. b

Exercise 11
1. en; 2. a, a; 3. en; 4. a; 5. de

Exercise 12
1. empezando; 2. salgo; 3. se parecen; 4. sueño;
5. me enfado; 6. acabo

Exercise 13
1. en; 2. a; 3. de; 4. por; 5. a; 6. en;
7. por; 8. en

Test 12

Exercise 1
1. a; 2. de; 3. a; 4. a; 5. en; 6. a; 7. en

Exercise 2
1. Los medios no dejan de dar la noticia.
2. El médico dice que debes dejar de fumar.
3. Ella no acaba de encontrar un buen puesto de trabajo.
4. El testigo se limitó a decir la verdad.
5. Luis parece simpático.
6. Mis vecinos se dedican a la carpintería.
7. Los lunes por la tarde baja a la calle a tomar el sol.
8. No quiere cambiar de piso todavía.

Exercise 3
1. c; 2. b; 3. d; 4. e; 5. a

Exercise 4
1. con; 2. a; 3. a; 4. en; 5. en;
6. con; 7. de; 8. a

§1 The Alphabet

Letters	Spanish Pronunciation	Letters	Spanish Pronunciation
a	a	n	ene
b	be	ñ	eñe
c	ce	o	o
ch	che, ce hache	p	pe
d	de	q	cu
e	e	r, rr	ere, erre
f	efe	s	ese
g	ge	t	te
h	hache	u	u
i	i	v	uve
j	jota	w	uve doble
k	ca	x	equis
l	ele	y	i griega
ll	elle	z	zeta
m	eme		

§2 Pronunciation

Letter	Placement	Pronunciation and Phonetic Symbol	Example
b und v	at beginning of word	[b] as in *boy*	**B**arcelona, **v**iaje
	between vowels	[β] softer, between **b** and **v**	Bolivia, La Habana
c	before **e, i**	[θ] lisped, as in *think* (Spain)*; elsewhere, like **s**	cerveza
	before **a, o, u**	[k] hard, as in *car*	Colombia, Cuba
ch		[tʃ] like **tch** in *chess*	Chile
g	before **e, i**	[x] guttural, as in initial sound of *chutzpah*	Argentina
gue/gui		[g] hard *g* as in *gold***	**Gui**tarra, **gue**rrilla
h		silent	hola
j		[x] guttural, as in initial sound of *chutzpah*	viaje
ll		[j] like initial sound of *yellow*	paella
ñ		[ɲ] like **gn** in *Cognac*	España
qu		[k] as in *car*	¿Qué tal? Quito
r	inside a word	[r] rolled with tip of tongue***	Perú, hora
	at beginning of word	rolled forcefully	Rosita
rr		[rr] rolled forcefully	guitarra
x		[ks] as in English	taxi
		otherwise: like Spanish **j**	México
y	at beginning of word and between vowels	[j] like initial sound of *yellow*	yo, playa
	otherwise	[i] as in *tipi*	soy, Chema y Jordi
z		[θ] lisped, as in *think* (Spain)*; elsewhere like **s**	cerveza

(*)   In Latin America and in certain regions of southern Spain (Andalusia, Canary Islands), this is pronounced as an **s** rather than lisped [θ].

(**) In certain words the **u** in **gue** or **gui** needs to be pronounced; in these cases this is indicated by two dots over the **u** (**la cigüeña**, the stork).

(***) The single Spanish **r** originates in the mouth rather than the throat. The tip of the tongue, placed near the upper front gums, vibrates briefly in the breath of air.

The Spanish language also has many dialectical shades and differences in pronunciation. However, they are not so great that they interfere with communication between the various Spanish-speaking countries.

 §3   Stress and Accent

1. Most Spanish words are stressed on the next to the last syllable. There are some words that end in a vowel, an **-n**, or an **-s**:
   amigo, **baños**, **examen**, **familia** (**-lia** counts as one syllable)
2. Words that end in a consonant other than **-n** or **-s** are stressed on the last syllable:
   español, **usted**, **señor**
3. Words that deviate from these rules require an accent that shows which syllable is stressed:
   sofá, **balcón**, **carácter**, **teléfono**
4. Question words in Spanish always have an accent:
   ¿Qué? ¿Dónde? ¿Cómo? – What? Where? How?
5. The accent is also used to distinguish between words with one syllable:

el – *the* (article)   **él** – *he* (personal pronoun)
tu – *your* (possessive adjective)   **tú** – *you* (personal pronoun)

6. When the syllable **-es** is added to form the plural of a word, the word gains or loses an accent so that the same syllable is stressed in the plural:

el catalán   **los catalanes**
the Catalonian   *the Catalonians*
el joven   **los jóvenes**
the youth   *the youths*

§4   Articles

1. The Definite Article

	masculine	feminine
Singular	**el**	**la**
Plural	**los**	**las**

Example: **el sombrero – los sombreros**
         the hat – the hats
         la casa – las casas
         the house – the houses

Note the following special case: when a feminine noun begins with a stressed *a*, the masculine **el** is used instead of the feminine definite article **la**. However, the word remains feminine. This serves merely to differentiate the definite article from the noun in the spoken language: **el agua** (feminine) – *the water*.

2. The Indefinite Article

	masculine	feminine
Singular	**un**	**una**
Plural	**unos**	**unas**

Example: **un español** (*a Spaniard*)
         una española (*a Spanish lady*)

The indefinite articles also have a plural form that refers to a non-specific quantity.
Example: **Tengo unos buenos amigos en Madrid.**
         I have (some) good friends in Madrid.

In Spanish, the indefinite article can be omitted in the plural:

Example: **Tengo buenos amigos en Madrid.**
I have good friends in Madrid.

§5 Nouns

In Spanish, nouns are either masculine or feminine.

Example: **la luna** – *the moon*; **el sol** – *the sun*

With respect to grammatical gender of nouns:
- Words that end in **-o** generally are masculine: **el apartamento** (*the apartment*), **el amigo** (*the friend*)
- Words that end in **-a** are generally feminine: **la hora** (*the hour*), **la amiga** (*the [female] friend*)
- Words that end in **-e** or a consonant can be either masculine or feminine: **el viaje** (*the trip*), **la mujer** (*the woman*)
- Words that end in **-dad** are feminine: **la verdad** (*the truth*)
- Words that end in **-ción** are feminine: **la información** (*the information*)
- Words that end in **-ema** are masculine: **el sistema** (*the system*), **el tema** (*the subject*)
- Words that designate people and end in **-ista** can be masculine or feminine: **el turista** (*the tourist*) / **la turista** (*the [female] tourist*)

There are also exceptions:
- Feminine nouns ending in **-o**: **la foto** (*the photo*), **la radio** (*the radio*), **la mano** (*the hand*), etc.
- Masculine nouns ending in **-a**: **el día** (*the day*)

To form the plural, an **-s** is added to nouns.
Example: **curso – cursos; hora – horas**

Nouns that end with a consonant add **-es** in the plural.
Example: **español – españoles; verdad – verdades**

§6 Adjectives

1. Adjectives agree in gender and number with the nouns they modify:
   Maite ha comprado una casa nueva.
   Maite has bought a new house.
   Ese chico es muy simpático.
   That boy is very nice.

2. Adjectives that end in **-o** change to a final **-a** for the feminine (the same rules for plural formation as with nouns apply):

	Singular	Plural
masculine	**un escritorio pequeño** *a small desk*	**escritorios pequeños** *small desks*
feminine	**una cocina pequeña** *a small kitchen*	**cocinas pequeñas** *small kitchens*

3. Adjectives that end in **-e** or a consonant have only one form for masculine and feminine (for plural formation the same rules as for nouns apply):

	Singular	Plural
masculine	**un piso grande** *a large apartment*	**pisos grandes** *large apartments*
feminine	**una cama grande** *a large bed*	**camas grandes** *large beds*

	Singular	Plural
masculine	**un viaje internacional** *an international trip*	**viajes internacionales** *international trips*
feminine	**una ciudad internacional** *an international city*	**ciudades internacionales** *international cities*

▼

4. Adjectives usually come after the nouns they modify:

¡Leo un libro muy interesante!
I am reading a very interesting book!

Some adjectives, however, can also come before the noun, for example, when a subjective evaluation is being expressed:

Es una bella mujer.
She is a beautiful woman.

Mucho, **poco**, and adjectives used in greetings and wishes are placed before the nouns:

Tengo mucho trabajo.
I have lots of work.

Hoy hay poco tráfico.
There's not much traffic today.

¡Buenos días!
Hello! Good morning!

¡Felices vacaciones!
Have a good vacation!

5. Some adjectives are shortened before a masculine singular noun:

bueno ▸ buen	un buen vino	
	a good wine	
malo ▸ mal	un mal estudiante	
	a bad student	

6. When an adjective refers to several nouns or persons of different gender, the masculine plural form is used:

¡El apartamento y la terraza son estupendos!
The apartment and terrace are great!

7. There may be differences in spelling or accent placement in the plural:

El niño está feliz. – *The child is happy.*
Los niños están felices. –
The children are happy.

  Chema es joven. – *Chema is young.*
  Chema y Jordi son jóvenes. –
  Chema and Jordi are young.

 § 7 Adjectives of Nationality / Designations of Profession

In Spanish, designations of nationality are always adjectives. Along with designations of profession, they are classified according to their ending:

– Words that end in **-o** or **-a** in the masculine or feminine form:

  mexicano / mexicana
  Mexican man / Mexican woman
  el ingeniero / la ingeniera
  the engineer (m. and f.)

– Words ending in a consonant that form the feminine by adding **-a**:

  español / española
  Spanish man / Spanish woman
  el profesor / la profesora
  the professor (m. and f.)

– Words ending in **-a** or **-e** remain the same:

  canadiense
  Canadian man / woman
  el estudiante / la estudiante
  the student (m. and f.)
  belga
  Belgian man / Belgian woman
  el taxista / la taxista
  the taxi driver (m. and f.)

The plural forms are constructed in the same way as with nouns:

mexicano-s	mexicana-s
español-es	española-s
canadiense-s	canadiense-s

Adjectives of nationality are always placed after the noun:

Chema es un chico español.
Chema is a Spanish boy.

In addition to the three classes of words mentioned previously, there is also the following pattern for adjectives of nationality:

iraní – *Iranian man / woman*
paquistaní – *Pakistani man / woman*
iraquí – *Iraqi man / woman*

§8 Diminutives

In Spanish, diminutive forms are very common and are very popular as nicknames. They are formed by adding the ending **-ito** or **-ita**:
¿Me pone una lechuguita (◄lechuga)?
Give me a small head of lettuce.

In this example it is noteworthy that **-g-** changes to **-gu-** to preserve the pronunciation.

With words that end in **-e** or a consonant, the ending **-cito/-cita** is used:
¿Tomamos un cafecito (◄café) aquí?
Shall we have a little coffee here?

You can deduce from this example that sometimes there are changes in the accents.

With words that have **-z-**, **-c-**, or **-g-** in the last syllable, the following spelling changes are used to preserve the pronunciation:
-z- ▶ **-c-** , for example, **terraza** ▶ **terracita**
-c- ▶ **-qu-**, for example, **un poco** ▶ **un poquito**
-g- ▶ **-gu-**, for example, **lechuga** ▶ **lechuguita**

§9 Adverbs

Whereas adjectives clarify nouns, adverbs clarify verbs, adjectives, other adjectives, or a whole clause.
For example:
In the sentence *That is a good restaurant*, the word *good* clarifies the noun (by telling what the restaurant is like); in other words, it is an adjective.
In the sentence *We eat well in this restaurant*, the word *well* clarifies the verb (by telling how we eat); in other words, it is an adverb.
In contrast to adjectives, adverbs are invariable.

1. Adverbs ending in *-mente*

In Spanish, adverbs can be formed from adjectives by adding the ending **-mente** to the feminine form of an adjective:
seguro/-a *(sure)* ▶ **segura**mente *(surely)*

When an adjective has only one form for masculine and feminine, the ending **-mente** is added directly:
fácil *(easy, simple)* ▶ **fácil**mente *(easily)*

N.B.: When the adjective has an accent, it is retained in the adverb form.

2. Irrregular Adverbs

Bien and **mal** are the adverbs that correspond to the adjectives **bueno/a** and **malo/a**:
Ellos se llevan bien.
They get along well.
Ese chico me cae mal.
I don't like that boy.

3. Adverbs and adverbial expressions of frequency:

siempre	*always*
normalmente	*normally*
con frecuencia	*frequently*
varias veces	*several times*
algunas veces	*sometimes*
a veces	*sometimes*
una vez	*once*
raramente	*rarely*
casi nunca	*almost never*
nunca	*never*
todos los días	*every day*
cada día	*every day*
una vez al día/ a la semana	*once a day / week*
una vez por día/ por semana*	*once a day / week*
dos veces al mes/ al año	*twice a month / a year*

▼

dos veces por mes / *twice a month /*
  por año* *a year*

* Instead of the preposition **a** the preposition
por can be used without an article:
una vez por año (*once a year*); however, the
preposition **a** is used more commonly.

§ 10 Comparatives

Equality:

> **tan + Adjective + como** *(as...as)*

**Para mí hacer deporte es <u>tan</u> importante
<u>como</u> salir con los amigos.**
*For me it's just as important to play sports as
to go out with friends.*

> **tanto/-a/-os/-as + noun + como**
> *(as many... as)*

Chema tiene <u>tantos</u> amigos <u>como</u> Jordi.
Chema has as many friends as Jordi.

Tanto/-a/-os/-as agrees in gender and number
with the noun it modifies.

Superiority:

> **más + adjective + que**

**Comer en la cantina es <u>más</u> práctico <u>que</u>
comer en casa.**
*It's more practical to eat in the cafeteria than
at home.*

Inferiority:

> **menos + adjective + que**

**Comer en casa es <u>menos</u> práctico <u>que</u> comer
en la cantina.**
*It's less practical to eat at home than in the
cafeteria.*

Some adjectives have irregular forms for compari-
sons of superiority, for example,
bueno/-a *(good)* ▸ **mejor** *(better)*
malo/-a *(bad)* ▸ **peor** *(worse)*

§ 11 Intensification

A very high degree or the highest degree of a
quality is expressed by using the adverb **muy** or
the ending **-ísimo/-a/-os/-as**, as demonstrated
by the following:
– With adjectives that end in a consonant,
  -ísimo is added directly:
  muy fácil ▸ **facilísimo** *very easy*
– With adjectives that end in a vowel, **-ísimo** is
  used instead of the final vowel:
  muy caro ▸ **carísimo** *very expensive*
  muy grande ▸ **grandísimo** *very big*

In order to preserve the pronunciation,
sometimes the spelling needs to be changed:
muy largo ▸ **larguísimo** *very long*
muy rico ▸ **riquísimo** *very rich*

Particularly expressive adjectives such as
fantástico do not use the ending **-ísimo**.
Instead, they can be intensified with **realmente**:
fantástico ▸ **realmente fantástico**
great ▸ *really great*

§ 12 *muy/mucho*

Muy *(very)* and **mucho** as an adverb *(much,
a lot)* are invariable.

Muy is placed before adjectives (for example,
amable) or adverbs (for example, **tarde**):
Es un chico muy amable.
He is a very nice boy.
¡Es muy tarde! – *It is very late!*

Mucho is placed after the verb to which it refers,
or is used alone:
Nos hemos divertido mucho.
We had a lot of fun.
¿Le ha gustado, abuela? – ¡Mucho!
Did you like it, grandmother? –Very much!

▼

Careful: **mucho** can also be used as an adjective; in this case, it agrees with the noun to which it refers:

Tengo muchas amigas en México.
I have lots of (girl) friends in Mexico.

 § 13 **Regular Verbs**

In Spanish, verbs are divided into three groups based on their infinitives:

1st conjugation: verbs ending in **-ar**
2nd conjugation: verbs ending in **-er**
3rd conjugation: verbs ending in **-ir**

The regular verbs are conjugated in the present tense as follows:

1. Regular verbs ending in *-ar*:

The following endings are added to the stem (that is, what's left over after dropping the **–ar** ending):

trabaj-ar *(to work)*

yo	trabaj-**o**	*I work*
tú	trabaj-**as**	*you work*
él, ella, usted	trabaj-**a**	*etc.*
nosotros, nosotras	trabaj-**amos**	
vosotros, vosotras	trabaj-**áis**	
ellos, ellas, ustedes	trabaj-**an**	

2. Regular verbs ending in *-er*:

The following endings are added to the verb stem:

com-er *(to eat)*

yo	com-**o**	*I eat*
tú	com-**es**	*you eat*
él, ella, usted	com-**e**	*etc.*
nosotros, nosotras	com-**emos**	
vosotros, vosotras	com-**éis**	
ellos, ellas, ustedes	com-**en**	

3. Regular verbs ending in *-ir*:

The following endings are added to the verb stem:

viv-ir *(to live)*

yo	viv-**o**	*I live*
tú	viv-**es**	*you live*
él, ella, usted	viv-**e**	*etc.*
nosotros, nosotras	viv-**imos**	
vosotros, vosotras	viv-**ís**	
ellos, ellas, ustedes	viv-**en**	

 § 14 **Irregular Verbs**

The irregular verbs are conjugated as follows in the present tense:

1. Verbs that are irregular in the first person singular:

estar *(to be, to be located)*

yo	**estoy**	*I am*
tú	**est-ás**	*you are*
él, ella, usted	**est-á**	*he, she, is, you are*
nosotros, nosotras	**est-amos**	*we are*
vosotros, vosotras	**est-áis**	*you are*
ellos, ellas, ustedes	**est-án**	*they / you are*

Here are some other verbs that are irregular in the first person singular:

hacer *(to make, do)* ▶ yo ha**g**o
poner *(to place, put)* ▶ yo pon**g**o
traer *(to bring)* ▶ yo trai**g**o
conocer *(to know a person, place, etc.)* ▶ yo cono**z**co
saber *(to know a fact, information, etc.)* ▶ yo **sé**
ver *(to see)* ▶ yo **veo**
▼

2. Irregular Stem-changing Verbs

With some verbs the stem vowel changes in the forms in which the stress falls on the stem (that is, all persons except for **nosotros** and **vosotros**):

e ▸ ie		

querer *(to want, to love)*

yo	qui**e**r-o	*I want*
tú	qui**e**r-es	*you want*
él, ella, usted	qui**e**r-e	*etc.*
nosotros, nosotras	quer-emos	
vosotros, vosotras	quer-éis	
ellos, ellas, ustedes	qui**e**r-en	

preferir *(to prefer)*

yo	prefi**e**r-o	*I prefer*
tú	prefi**e**r-es	*you prefer*
él, ella, usted	prefi**e**r-e	*etc.*
nosotros, nosotras	prefer-imos	
vosotros, vosotras	prefer-ís	
ellos, ellas, ustedes	prefi**e**r-en	

This also applies to the following verbs:
empezar *(to begin)*
pensar *(to think)*
sentirse *(to feel)*

o ▸ ue		

poder *(to be able, can, may)*

yo	pu**e**d-o	*I can*
tú	pu**e**d-es	*you can*
él, ella, usted	pu**e**d-e	*etc.*
nosotros, nosotras	pod-emos	
vosotros, vosotras	pod-éis	
ellos, ellas, ustedes	pu**e**-den	

It likewise applies to the following verbs:
almorzar *(to have lunch)*
acostarse *(to lie down)*
dormir *(to sleep)*
doler *(to hurt)*

Please note: the verb **doler** is used with indirect object pronouns:
Me duele la mano. – *My hand hurts.*

e ▸ i		

seguir *(to follow, to continue)*

yo	sig-o	*I continue*
tú	sigu-es	*you continue*
él, ella, usted	sigu-e	*etc.*
nosotros, nosotras	segu-imos	
vosotros, vosotras	segu-ís	
ellos, ellas, ustedes	sigu-en	

This also applies to the following verbs:
conseguir *(to achieve, obtain)*
elegir *(to choose, select)*
freír *(to fry)*
pedir *(to order, ask for)*
repetir *(to repeat)*
servir *(to serve)*
vestir *(to dress)*

With the verbs **seguir**, **conseguir**, and **elegir** it is also to be noted that there is a spelling change to maintain the pronunciation.
-gu- ▸ **-g-:**   se**gu**ir ▸ si**g**o
               conse**gu**ir ▸ consi**g**o
-g- ▸ **-j-:**   ele**g**ir ▸ eli**j**o

3. Mixed Verbs:

These verbs not only have an irregular first person singular, but also a vowel change in the stem.

tener *(to have)*

yo	ten**g**-o	*I have*
tú	ti**e**n-es	*you have*
él, ella, usted	ti**e**n-e	*etc.*
nosotros, nosotras	ten-emos	
vosotros, vosotras	ten-éis	
ellos, ellas, ustedes	ti**e**n-en	

▼

decir *(to say)*

yo	d**ig**-o	*I say*
tú	dic-es	*you say*
él, ella, usted	dic-e	*etc.*
nosotros, nosotras	dec-imos	
vosotros, vosotras	dec-ís	
ellos, ellas, ustedes	d**ic**-en	

4. Very Irregular Verbs

ser *(to be)*

yo	**soy**	*I am*
tú	**eres**	*you are*
él, ella, usted	**es**	*etc.*
nosotros, nosotras	**somos**	
vosotros, vosotras	**sois**	
ellos, ellas, ustedes	**son**	

ir *(to go)*

yo	**voy**	*I go*
tú	**vas**	*you go*
él, ella, usted	**va**	*etc.*
nosotros, nosotras	**vamos**	
vosotros, vosotras	**vais**	
ellos, ellas, ustedes	**van**	

 § 15 The Perfect Tense / Form and Usage

1. Form

The perfect consists of two parts:
A form of the verb **haber** + a past participle (invariable)
for example, **he   trabajado**
         I have   worked

The **-ar** verbs (for example, **trabajar**) form their past participle with the ending **-ado** (for example, **trabajado**). Verbs ending in **-er** and **-ir** (for example, **comer**, **vivir**) form the past participle with the ending **-ido** (for example, **comido**, **vivido**)

Here is the complete conjugation:

yo	**he**	*have*	**trabaj<u>ado</u>**
tú	**has**	*have*	*worked*
él, ella, usted	**ha**	*has*	**com<u>ido</u>**
nosotros, nosotras	**hemos**	*have*	*eaten*
vosotros, vosotras	**habéis**	*have*	**viv<u>ido</u>**
ellos, ellas, ustedes	**han**	*have*	*lived*

The following are some irregular past participle forms:

abrir	▶	**abierto** *(opened)*
decir	▶	**dicho** *(said)*
escribir	▶	**escrito** *(written)*
hacer	▶	**hecho** *(done, made)*
poner	▶	**puesto** *(put, placed)*
ver	▶	**visto** *(seen)*
volver	▶	**vuelto** *(returned)*

When a verb is accompanied by a pronoun (whether direct, indirect, or reflexive) in the perfect, the pronoun comes immediately before the verb:
¿Has visto a la abuela en el bar de Paco?
Did you see the grandmother in Paco's bar?
Sí, <u>la</u> he visto. *Yes, I saw her.*

In a negative construction, the **no** comes not immediately before the verb, but rather before the pronoun:
No, <u>no la</u> he visto.
No, I didn't see her.

2. Usage

The perfect is a past-tense form with a close relationship to present time. Thus it is used in combination with time expressions that refer to the present moment or time frame: **hoy** *(today)*, **esta mañana** *(this morning)*, **esta semana** *(this week)*, **este año** *(this year)*.

¿Qué has hecho hoy?
What did you do today?

▼

Este año he trabajado mucho.
I (have) worked a lot this year.

In addition, the perfect is used for events whose timing is not specified or significant, for example, **alguna vez** (*sometime*), **todavía no** (*not yet*), **muchas veces** (*frequently*), **nunca** (*never*).

¿Has estado alguna vez en Managua?
Have you ever been in Managua?
No hemos ido nunca a San Juan.
We have never gone to San Juan.

 §16   The Indefinido / Form and Usage

1. Form

Regular Forms

Verbs ending in **-ar**:

yo	**trabaj-é**	*I was working*
tú	**trabaj-aste**	*you were working*
él, ella, usted	**trabaj-ó**	*etc.*
nosotros, nosotras	**trabaj-amos**	
vosotros, vosotras	**trabaj-asteis**	
ellos, ellas, ustedes	**trabaj-aron**	

Verbs ending in **-er**:

yo	**com-í**	*I was eating*
tú	**com-iste**	*you were eating*
él, ella, usted	**com-ió**	*etc.*
nosotros, nosotras	**com-imos**	
vosotros, vosotras	**com-isteis**	
ellos, ellas, ustedes	**com-ieron**	

Verbs ending in **-ir**:

yo	**viv-í**	*I was living*
tú	**viv-iste**	*you were living*
él, ella, usted	**viv-ió**	*etc.*
nosotros, nosotras	**viv-imos**	
vosotros, vosotras	**viv-isteis**	
ellos, ellas, ustedes	**viv-ieron**	

Irregular Forms

ser and **ir**
In the indefinido, these two verbs have the same forms (the meaning in each case becomes clear from the context).

yo	**fui**	*I was / was going*
tú	**fuiste**	*you were / were going*
él, ella, usted	**fue**	*etc.*
nosotros, nosotras	**fuimos**	
vosotros, vosotras	**fuisteis**	
ellos, ellas, ustedes	**fueron**	

Verbs with an irregular stem (however, the same endings are used for all of them):

tener

yo	**tuv-e**	*I had*
tú	**tuv-iste**	*you had*
él, ella, usted	**tuv-o**	*etc.*
nosotros, nosotras	**tuv-imos**	
vosotros, vosotras	**tuv-isteis**	
ellos, ellas, ustedes	**tuv-ieron**	

estar

yo	**estuv-e**	*I was*
tú	**estuv-iste**	*you were*
él, ella, usted	**estuv-o**	*etc.*
nosotros, nosotras	**estuv-imos**	
vosotros, vosotras	**estuv-isteis**	
ellos, ellas, ustedes	**estuv-ieron**	

saber

yo	**sup-e**	*I knew*
tú	**sup-iste**	*you knew*
él, ella, usted	**sup-o**	*etc.*
nosotros, nosotras	**sup-imos**	
vosotros, vosotras	**sup-isteis**	
ellos, ellas, ustedes	**sup-ieron**	

poder

yo	**pud**-e	*I was able*
tú	**pud**-iste	*you were able*
él, ella, usted	**pud**-o	*tc.*
nosotros, nosotras	**pud**-imos	
vosotros, vosotras	**pud**-isteis	
ellos, ellas, ustedes	**pud**-ieron	

poner

yo	**pus**-e	*I placed*
tú	**pus**-iste	*you placed*
él, ella, usted	**pus**-o	*etc.*
nosotros, nosotras	**pus**-imos	
vosotros, vosotras	**pus**-isteis	
ellos, ellas, ustedes	**pus**-ieron	

The verb **proponer** (*to suggest, propose*) is conjugated like **poner**.

Note: the indefinido of **hay** (*there is, there are*) is **hubo**.

querer

yo	**quis**-e	*I wanted*
tú	**quis**-iste	*you wanted*
él, ella, usted	**quis**-o	*etc.*
nosotros, nosotras	**quis**-imos	
vosotros, vosotras	**quis**-isteis	
ellos, ellas, ustedes	**quis**-ieron	

venir

yo	**vin**-e	*I came*
tú	**vin**-iste	*you came*
él, ella, usted	**vin**-o	*etc.*
nosotros, nosotras	**vin**-imos	
vosotros, vosotras	**vin**-isteis	
ellos, ellas, ustedes	**vin**-ieron	

hacer (in the third person singular there is a spelling change: **c ▸ z**)

yo	**hic**-e	*I made / did*
tú	**hic**-iste	*you made / did*
él, ella, usted	**hiz**-o	*etc.*
nosotros, nosotras	**hic**-imos	
vosotros, vosotras	**hic**-isteis	
ellos, ellas, ustedes	**hic**-ieron	

decir (in the third person plural a letter is left out of the ending: **-ieron ▸ -eron**)

yo	**dij**-e	*I said*
tú	**dij**-iste	*you said*
él, ella, usted	**dij**-o	*etc.*
nosotros, nosotras	**dij**-imos	
vosotros, vosotras	**dij**-isteis	
ellos, ellas, ustedes	**dij**-eron	

This also applies to the verb **traer**:

yo	**traj**-e	*I brought*
tú	**traj**-iste	*you brought*
él, ella, usted	**traj**-o	*etc.*
nosotros, nosotras	**traj**-imos	
vosotros, vosotras	**traj**-isteis	
ellos, ellas, ustedes	**traj**-eron	

With verbs ending in **ir** that experience a vowel change in the present (for example, **pedir ▸ (yo) pido, divertirse ▸ (yo) me divierto**), the stem vowel also changes from **e** to **i** in the indefinido, but only in the third persons singular and plural:

yo	**ped**-í	*I ordered*
tú	**ped**-iste	*you ordered*
él, ella, usted	**pid**-ió	*etc.*
nosotros, nosotras	**ped**-imos	
vosotros, vosotras	**ped**-isteis	
ellos, ellas, ustedes	**pid**-ieron	

This also applies to the verb **divertirse** (*to have fun, amuse oneself*).

▼

With **-ir** verbs that have a vowel change from **o ▶ ue** (e.g. **dormir ▶ (yo) d<u>ue</u>rmo**), in the indefinido the stem vowel always changes from **o** to **u**, but only in the third persons singular and plural:

yo	**dorm-í**	*I sleep*
tú	**dorm-iste**	*you sleep*
él, ella, usted	**d<u>u</u>rm-ió**	*etc.*
nosotros, nosotras	**dorm-imos**	
vosotros, vosotras	**dorm-isteis**	
ellos, ellas, ustedes	**d<u>u</u>rm-ieron**	

Some verbs change their spelling in the indefinido to preserve the pronunciation. Thus **c**, **z**, or **g** at the end of a word stem change to **qu**, **c**, or **gu** before the **e** of the first person singular:

buscar

yo	**bus<u>qu</u>-é**	*I sought*
tú	**busc-aste**	*you sought*
él, ella, usted	**busc-ó**	*etc.*
nosotros, nosotras	**busc-amos**	
vosotros, vosotras	**busc-asteis**	
ellos, ellas, ustedes	**busc-aron**	

empezar

yo	**empe<u>c</u>-é**	*I began*
tú	**empez-aste**	*you began*
él, ella, usted	**empez-ó**	*etc.*
nosotros, nosotras	**empez-amos**	
vosotros, vosotras	**empez-asteis**	
ellos, ellas, ustedes	**empez-aron**	

llegar

yo	**lle<u>gu</u>-é**	*I arrived*
tú	**lleg-aste**	*you arrived*
él, ella, usted	**lleg-ó**	*etc.*
nosotros, nosotras	**lleg-amos**	
vosotros, vosotras	**lleg-asteis**	
ellos, ellas, ustedes	**lleg-aron**	

There is a change from **i ▶ y** in the vowel of the ending with some verbs such as **leer**, but only in the third persons singular and plural:

yo	**le-í**	*I read*
tú	**le-íste**	*you read*
él, ella, usted	**le-<u>y</u>ó**	*etc.*
nosotros, nosotras	**le-ímos**	
vosotros, vosotras	**le-ísteis**	
ellos, ellas, ustedes	**le-<u>y</u>eron**	

Note the accent on the **i**.

This also applies to the verb **creer** (*to believe*).

2. Usage

The indefinido expresses actions or events that the speaker considers to be completed. Thus, the indefinido often is used in conjunction with expressions of time, such as **el otro día** (*the other day*), **ayer** (*yesterday*), **la semana pasada** (*last week*), **el mes pasado** (*last month*),**el año pasado** (*last year*), and **en 1970** (*in 1970*).
El otro día vi a Rosita en el médico y hablamos un rato.
I saw Rosita at the doctor's office the other day, and we talked for a while.

The indefinido is used in some regions of Spain and in most countries of Latin America in place of the perfect:
¿Adónde <u>fuiste</u> hoy?/¿Adónde <u>has ido</u> hoy?
Where did you go today? / Where have you gone today?

 § 17   The Imperfect / Form and Usage

1. Form

The imperfect (**imperfecto**) is another past-tense verb form.

Regular Forms

Verbs ending in **-ar** (for example, **trabaj-ar**):

yo	**trabaj-aba**
tú	**trabaj-abas**
él, ella, usted	**trabaj-aba**
nosotros, nosotras	**trabaj-ábamos**
vosotros, vosotras	**trabaj-abais**
ellos, ellas, ustedes	**trabaj-aban**

Verbs ending in **-er** and **-ir** (for example, **com-er / viv-ir**):

yo	**com-ía / viv-ía**
tú	**com-ías / viv-ías**
él, ella, usted	**com-ía / viv-ía**
nosotros, nosotras	**com-íamos / viv-íamos**
vosotros, vosotras	**com-íais / viv-íais**
ellos, ellas, ustedes	**com-ían / viv-ían**

Irregular Forms

ser	ver	ir
era	veía	iba
eras	veías	ibas
era	veía	iba
éramos	veíamos	íbamos
erais	veíais	ibais
eran	veían	iban

The imperfect of **hay** (*there is / there are*) is **había**.

2. Usage

The imperfect is used to describe situations, conditions, and circumstances in past time. Note the following examples:
- to describe a condition:
  ¡Estábamos preocupadísimas!
  We were extremely worried!
- to describe a condition or circumstance:
  El restaurante era precioso.
  The restaurant was very nice.
- to describe a person:
  Tenía los ojos azules.
  He / she had blue eyes.
- to describe a situation:
  Hacía mucho calor.
  It was very hot out.
- to describe a situation that forms the background or the condition for a new occurrence (the new occurrence is in the indefinido or the perfect tense):
  La temperatura <u>era</u> muy agradable, <u>había</u> mucha gente en la plaza y el grupo musical <u>era</u> excelente, así que decidimos sentarnos en una terraza y tomar algo.
  The temperature was very pleasant, there were lots of people in the square, and the band was excellent. So we decided to sit on a terraza and have something to drink.
- to describe repeated and habitual actions in past time:
  Cuando tenía tu edad, <u>iba</u> a bailar a las verbenas.
  When I was your age, I (always) went to the open-air dances.

The imperfect is often used with specifications such as **antes** (*formerly*), **siempre** (*always*), **todos los días** (*every day*), **mientras** (*while*), etc. The indefinido that is used to specify the new occurrence is often used with specifications such as **entonces** (*then*), **de repente** (*suddenly*), **de pronto** (*suddenly*), **enseguida** (*immediately*), **un día** (*one day*), etc.

§ 18 Present Participle / Form and Usage

1. Form

The present participle is easily derived from the infinitive:
Verbs ending in **-ar** change their ending to **-ando**;
Verbs ending in **-er** and **-ir** change their ending to **-iendo**:

trabaj<u>ar</u>	▶	trabaj<u>ando</u>
com<u>er</u>	▶	com<u>iendo</u>
viv<u>ir</u>	▶	viv<u>iendo</u>

There are a few irregular present participle forms:
- A change in the stem vowel from **e** ▸ **i** (as in the present-tense forms of the corresponding verbs):
  decir ▸ **d<u>i</u>ciendo**
- A change in the stem vowel from **o** ▸ **u**:
  dormir ▸ **d<u>u</u>rmiendo**
- When the verb stem ends in a vowel, the ending **-iendo** changes to **-yendo**:
  leer ▸ **le<u>y</u>endo**

This also happens with the verb **ir** ▸ **yendo**.

2. Usage

In describing an action that is occurring right now, the structure **estar** + present participle is used:

¡Estoy preparando algo de cena!
I am preparing something for dinner!

If the sentence contains a pronoun, it comes either before the verb **estar** or is appended to the present participle. In this case an accent is required to preserve the stress:

<u>Le</u> **estoy escribiendo una carta. = Estoy escribiéndo<u>le</u> una carta.**
I am (in the process of) writing him a letter.

¿<u>Te</u> estás afeitando, Agustín? = ¿Estás afeitándo<u>te</u>, Agustín?
Are you shaving (now), Agustín?

The present participle can also be used alone and then takes the place of a subordinate clause (*when, if...*):

Comiendo en la cafetería se ahorra tiempo y dinero.
By eating in the cafeteria you will save time and money.

The present participle is very frequently used in combination with the verbs **pasar** (*to spend*) and **seguir** (*to follow*):

Yo siempre paso las tardes leyendo.
I always spend the afternoons reading.
Vamos a seguir buscando.
We'll continue looking.

 § 19 *Ser / estar*

Ser is used in the following instances:
- To provide name and identity:
  Yo soy Chema. *I am Chema.*
  Esta es mi hermana. *This is my sister.*
- To specify origin or nationality:
  Rosita es mexicana. *Rosita is Mexican.*
- To specify profession or position:
  Agustín es jefe del departamento de ventas.
  Agustín is the head of the sales department.
- To specify characteristic traits of people and things (description):
  Chema y Jordi son muy simpáticos.
  Chema and Jordi are very nice.
  México es un país fantástico.
  Mexico is a wonderful country.
- For telling time:
  Es la una y media. *It is one-thirty.*
  Son las ocho. *It is eight o'clock.*

Estar is used for the following:
- geographic or physical location:
  El bolso está encima de la mesa.
  The bag is on top of the table.
- telling how a person feels:
  ¿Cómo está usted? *How are you?*
- temporary or changeable conditions and qualities:
  La habitación está desordenada.
  The room is messy.
  Estoy muy contenta en Madrid.
  I am very happy in Madrid.
- assessments of food and drink
  Estas naranjas están muy ricas.
  These oranges are very delicious.
- with the adverb **bien**:
  ¿Está bien así? *Is that OK?*

Note that some adjectives have a different meaning depending on whether they are used with **ser** or **estar**:
ser cansado/-a – *to be tiring, strenuous*
estar cansado/-a – *to be tired*

§20 Hay/está or están

Hay corresponds to the English *there is / there are* and is an invariable present tense form of the verb **haber** (*to have*).

It is used when there is no reference to a specific thing or person.
Thus, **hay** comes
- before the indefinite article:
  En esta casa hay <u>un</u> ladrón.
  There is a thief in this house.
- before plural words with no article:
  En Oaxaca hay <u>museos</u> interesantes.
  In Oaxaca there are (some) interesting museums.
- before counting words:
  Encima de la mesa hay <u>dos</u> bolígrafos.
  There are two pens on the table.

The forms **está/están** are used in speaking of a specific person or thing. Thus, these forms come before the definite article or before the possessive adjective:
¿Dónde está <u>la</u> abuela?
Where is the grandmother?
Aquí están <u>la</u> agenda y <u>el</u> celular.
Here are the appointment calendar and the cell phone.
¿Dónde está <u>tu</u> hermano?
Where is your brother?

§21 Reflexive Verbs

Reflexive verbs are recognizable by the infinitive ending **-se**, for example, **ducharse** (*to take a shower*), **llamarse** (*to be called / named*). They require the use of a reflexive pronoun (*myself, yourself, himself, etc.*).
They consist of the reflexive pronoun and the verb form corresponding to each person:

yo	<u>me</u>	**llamo**	*My name is*
tú	<u>te</u>	**llamas**	*your name is*
él, ella, usted	<u>se</u>	**llama**	*etc.*
nosotros, nosotras	<u>nos</u>	**llamamos**	
vosotros, vosotras	<u>os</u>	**llamáis**	
ellos, ellas, ustedes	<u>se</u>	**llaman**	

Note that some verbs are reflexive in Spanish but not in English, for example, **levantarse** (*to get up*) and **llamarse** (*to be called / named*).

§22 The Impersonal Form se

In general statements in Spanish the impersonal third person **se** (= *one / people / they*) is used. The verb is used in the third person, either singular or plural, depending on whether the subject of the sentence is singular or plural:
En ese bar <u>se come</u> un jamón muy bueno.
They serve a very fine ham in that bar.
En ese bar <u>se comen</u> unas croquetas muy ricas.
They serve some very delicious croquettes in that bar.

§23 Infinitive Constructions

es + adjective + infinitive

Impersonal expressions can be conveyed with the structure **(no) es + adjective + infinitive**:
Es importante descansar.
It is important to rest.

hay que + infinitive

This impersonal expression is used to express obligation or necessity in an impersonal form:
Hay que dormir 7 horas como mínimo.
It is necessary to sleep a minimum of 7 hours.

Note: A duty or necessity is also expressed with **tener que** + infinitive, but in this case the subject must be named, so it cannot be used as in an impersonal expression:

▼

Tienes que trabajar menos.
You must / have to work less.

---

querer *(to want)* **+ infinitive**

This structure is used to express a desire or an intention.
¿Qué quieres tomar?
What do you want to drink?
En abril quiero visitar Sevilla.
In April I want to visit Sevilla.

---

ir a **+ infinitive**

This structure is used to express an intention or plan in the near future:
Mañana voy a dar un paseo con mis amigas.
Tomorrow I am going to take a walk with my girlfriends.

---

pensar **+ infinitive**

This structure is used to express an intention or a plan:
También pienso ahorrar un poquito...
I also plan to save a little money...

---

§ 24 Negation

No is always placed before the verb and the reflexive, direct object, and indirect object pronouns, and can be translated as *not*:
¿Vives en Acapulco? – No, vivo en Oaxaca.
Do you live in Acapulco? – No, I live in Oaxaca.
Yo no me llamo María, sino Marisa.
My name is not María, but Marisa.
Félix no tiene dinero. *Felix has no money.*

Please note the following difference:

| **No, soy de México.** | **No soy de México.** |
| *No, I am from Mexico.* | *I am not from Mexico.* |

In pronunciang the sentence **No, soy de México** there must be a pause after the no (because of the comma); otherwise, the sentence is negated.

Double Negation

With words like **nada** (*nothing*), **ningún / ninguno / ninguna** (*no, not any, none*), **nunca** (*never*), and **ni...ni** (*neither...nor*), double negatives are permissible in Spanish when these expressions come after the verb:
<u>No</u> quiero beber <u>nada</u>, gracias.
I don't want anything to drink, thanks.
<u>No</u> me gusta <u>ninguna</u> falda de esa tienda.
I don't like any of the skirts in that shop.
<u>No</u> he estado <u>nunca</u> en México.
I have never been in Mexico.
<u>No</u> tomo <u>ni</u> café <u>ni</u> té.
I drink neither coffee nor tea.

---

§ 25 Subject Pronouns

The subject pronouns are:

Singular	1st Person	**yo**	*I*
	2nd Person	**tú**	*you (informal)*
	3rd Person	**él, ella, usted**	*he, she, you (formal)*
Plural	1st Person	**nosotros, nosotras**	*we*
	2nd Person	**vosotros, vosotras**	*you (informal)*
	3rd Person	**ellos, ellas, ustedes**	*they, you (formal)*

In the polite form of address there is a singular (**usted**, abbreviated to **Ud.**) and a plural (**ustedes**, abbreviated to **Uds.**), depending on whether we are addressing one or more people.

The personal pronouns **nosotros**, **vosotros** also have the corresponding feminine forms **nosotras**, **vosotras**.

In Spanish, subject pronouns are used only in the following instances:
- to stress a particular person or to set someone apart from others
- to avoid misunderstandings

Example: **<u>Yo</u> soy Chema y éste es Jordi.**
          I am Chema and this is Jordi.

In Latin-American countries, **ustedes** is always used instead of **vosotros**, so in the plural the informal and formal forms are the same:
Example: (Latin-America)
          Ustedes son Chema y Jordi, ¿verdad?
          You are Chema and Jordi, right?

 § 26 Direct Object Pronouns

me	*me*
te	*you*
lo	*him, it, you (formal, m.)*
la	*her, it, you (formal, f.)*
nos	*us*
os	*you (informal, pl.)*
los, las	*them, you (formal, pl.)*

The direct object pronouns agree in gender and number with the words they stand for and always come immediately before the verb:

¿Dónde están <u>las gafas</u>? No <u>las</u> veo.
Where are the glasses? I don't see them.

Lo can also refer to a whole sentence or a question:

¿Sabes <u>dónde está mi monedero</u>? – No, no <u>lo</u> sé, mamá.
Do you know where my wallet is? – No, that I don't know, mom.

When the direct object precedes the verb, it must be repeated in the form of a direct object pronoun. This pronoun agrees in gender and number with the word to which it refers.

Este impermeable <u>lo</u> utilizo sólo para lluvias fuertes.
I use this raincoat only for torrential rain.

§ 27 Indirect Object Pronouns

Non-accentuating Indirect Object Pronouns

me	*to / for me*
te	*to / for you*
le	*to / for him, her, you (formal)*
nos	*to / for us*
os	*to / for you (pl., informal)*
les	*to / for them, you (pl.)*

The indirect object pronouns are always placed immediately before the verb:
¿Qué le muestro? *What can I show you?*

Accentuating Indirect Object Pronouns

a mí	*to / for me*
a ti	*to / for you*
a él, a ella	*to / for him, her*
a usted	*to / for you (formal)*
a nosotros, a nosotras	*to / for us*
a vosotros, a vosotras	*to / for you (pl.)*
a ellos, a ellas	*to / for them*
a ustedes	*to / for you (pl. fam. or formal)*

It is possible for a sentence to contain two indirect objects. In addition to the non-accentuating pronouns (**me**, **te**, **le**, **nos**, **os**, **les**), which are required, the accentuating indirect object pronouns can also be used:
A mí me encantan los cosméticos.
I love makeup.

Instead of the accentuating indirect object pronoun, the sentence can contain an indirect object (for example, a name):

▼

¿A Noelia le gustan los cosméticos?
Does Noelia like cosmetics?

This repetition is used to emphasize the person and avoids misunderstandings (especially in the third person).

Indirect Object Pronouns after the Prepositions *para* and *con*:

para mí	*for me*
para ti	*for you*
para él, ella, usted	*for him, her, you (formal)*
para nosotros, nosotras	*for us*
para vosotros, vosotras	*for you (fam. pl.)*
para ellos, ellas, ustedes	*for them, you (pl.)*
conmigo	*with me*
contigo	*with you*
con él, ella, usted	*with him, her, you (formal)*
con nosotros, nosotras	*with us*
con vosotros, vosotras	*with you (fam. pl.)*
con ellos, ellas, ustedes	*with them, you (pl.)*

Indirect Object Pronouns with the Verbs *encantar* and *gustar*:

The verbs **encantar** (*to enchant, to love*) and **gustar** (*to like, to like to do*) are used with indirect object pronouns and agree with the subject (the person or thing that is pleasing):
¡Me encanta México! *I love Mexico!*
Me encantan los baños grandes.
I love large bathrooms.
¿Te gusta viajar? *Do you like to travel?*
¿Te gustan los muebles?
 Do you like the furniture?

§ 28 Combinations of Pronouns

If both an indirect and a direct object pronoun are used in a single sentence, the indirect comes before the direct. Both are placed before the verb:
Si no tienes dinero, te lo dejo yo.
If you don't have any money I will lend you some.

The indirect object pronouns **le / les** change to **se** when the direct object pronoun **lo / la / los / las** follows:
¿Le has comprado ya el regalo a tu madre?
No, todavía no se lo he comprado.
Have you already bought the gift for your mother? No, I haven't bought it for her yet.

§ 29 Pronoun Placement

Direct, indirect, and reflexive pronouns generally come before the verb. However, with compound tenses they are placed before the verb **haber**:
¿Has visto a la abuela en el bar de Paco? Sí, la he visto.
Have you seen the grandmother in Paco's bar? Yes, I have seen her.

With present participles and infinitive constructions, such as with modal verbs like **poder** + infinitive, or **tener que** + infinitive, the pronouns may either come before the infinitive or be added to the participle:
¿Le puedo ayudar en algo? = ¿Puedo ayudarle en algo?
May I help you with something?

With attached pronouns, an accent must be added to preserve the pronunciation:
Quiere dármelo mañana.
He wants to give it to me tomorrow.

§ 30 The Dative of Interest

In Spanish, the so-called **dativo de interés** is an indirect object pronoun that is used to indicate the speaker's involvement in something that has happened to him / her or another person. It expresses the speaker's perplexity and inner sympathy with the occurrence. In English it is difficult to convey this nuance in the meaning of the sentence, and so the following two sentences would be translated in the same way.

¡Se me ha colgado el ordenador! = ¡Se ha colgado el ordenador!
My computer has crashed!

 §31 Direct Objects

When the direct object is a person or a group of people, it is preceded by the preposition **a**, whether they are named specifically or represented by pronouns (for example, **nadie**, **quién**, **alguien**):

¿Has visto a la abuela?
Did you see the grandmother?
¿Han ustedes visto a alguien?
Did you see somebody?

In all other cases the direct object immediately follows the verb:

¿Has visto la película?
Have you seen the film?

The preposition **a** is omitted with the verbs **buscar** and **necesitar** in combination with professional designations, plus with nouns with an indefinite article after the verb **tener**:

La empresa busca una secretaria.
The company is looking for a secretary.
Yo tengo una hermana.
I have a sister.

 §32 Indefinite Pronouns

The pronoun **uno** (*one*) corresponds to the indefinite article un without a noun:

Cuando tenía tu edad, tenía muchos novios: uno para el lunes, otro para el martes, otro para el ...
When I was your age, I had lots of boyfriends: one for Monday, another for Tuesday, a different one for...

The feminine form and the plural correspond to the indefinite article:

No tengo aspirinas. ¿Tienes tú una?
I don't have any aspirins. Do you have one?
Yo siempre llevo gemelos. Ayer me regalaron unos de oro. *I always wear cufflinks. Yesterday I was given some gold ones.*
Yo no necesito botas de montaña. Ya tengo unas. *I don't need mountain-climbing boots. I already have some.*

 §33 Demonstrative Adjectives and Pronouns

The demonstratives designate specific objects or people that are in the immediate vicinity of the speaker: **este / esta / estos / estas** – or farther away – **ese / esa / esos / esas**.

	Singular	Plural
masculine	**este libro** *this book (here)*	**estos libros** *these books (here)*
	ese libro *that book (there)*	**esos libros** *those books (there)*
feminine	**esta casa** *this house (here)*	**estas casas** *these houses (here)*
	esa casa *that house (there)*	**esas casas** *those houses (there)*

The demonstrative adjectives can be used in combination with nouns or stand alone. In the latter case they may have a written accent.

¿Te gusta este bote?
Do you like this boat (here)?
¿Ése? Sí, es bastante bonito.
That one (there)? Yes, it's quite nice.

In certain cases where ambiguity would otherwise result, an accent is required:

Dice que <u>ésta</u> (= *a woman*) **mañana no tiene tiempo.**
He says that this woman has no time tomorrow.
Esto and **eso** are never used in combination with a noun. They refer to something that is not named specifically or that remains to be defined:

¿Qué es esto?   *What is this (here)?*
No entiendo eso.   *I don't understand that.*

§34 Possessive Adjectives and Pronouns

1. The Non-accentuating Possessives

The non-accentuating possessives generally come before the nouns.

Masculine

mi	**abuelo**	*my grandfather*
tu	**abuelo**	*your grandfather*
su	**abuelo**	*his, her, your (formal) grandfather*
nuestro	**abuelo**	*our grandfather*
vuestro	**abuelo**	*your (fam. pl.) grandfather*
su	**abuelo**	*their, your (pl., formal and informal) grandfather*

Feminine

mi	**abuela**	*my grandmother*
tu	**abuela**	*your grandmother*
su	**abuela**	*his, her, your (formal) grandmother*
nuestra	**abuela**	*our grandmother*
vuestra	**abuela**	*your (fam. pl.) grandmother*
su	**abuela**	*heir, your (pl., formal and informal) grandmother*

The forms of the possessive adjectives are the same for masculine and feminine, except for **nuestro / nuestra** and **vuestro / vuestra**, which agree in gender and number with the object possessed.

The possessive adjectives agree in number with the object possessed. To form the plural, an **-s** is added:
Tus padres están con mis abuelos.
Your parents are with my grandparents.

2. The Accentuating Possessives

The accentuating possessives are used to avoid repeating a previously mentioned noun. The possessive is then used with a definite article:
Tú tienes a tu <u>familia</u> cerca, ¡y <u>la mía</u> está tan lejos!
Your family is close to you, and mine is so far away!

When asking about the owner, no article is used before the possessive:
¿Son <u>tuyas</u> estas gafas? – Sí, son <u>mías</u>.
Are these your glasses? – Yes, they are mine.

The accentuating forms can also come after a noun if the thing possessed is stressed:
Yo no conozco a esas amigas <u>tuyas</u>.
I don't know those friends of yours.

In certain exclamations the accentuating possessives are used after nouns:
¡Dios <u>mío</u>!	*My God!*
Hijo <u>mío</u>	*My son*
Amigo <u>mío</u>	*My friend*

When one of several is meant, the possessive follows the noun and the corresponding indefinite article:
Ese chico es <u>un colega mío</u>.
That young man is a colleague of mine.

Here are the forms:

Masculine

mío(s)	*mine*
tuyo(s)	*yours*
suyo(s)	*his, hers, yours (formal)*
nuestro(s)	*ours*
vuestro(s)	*yours (fam. pl.)*
suyo(s)	*theirs, yours (pl., fam. and formal)*

▼

Feminine

mía(s)	*mine*
tuya(s)	*yours*
suya(s)	*his, hers, yours (formal)*
nuestra(s)	*ours*
vuestra(s)	*yours (pl., fam.)*
suya(s)	*theirs, yours (pl., fam. and formal)*

 §35 Relative Pronouns

The relative pronoun **que** (*which, that*) is used for masculine and feminine objects and persons in both singular and plural, as the subject or direct object:

Tenemos un vino de California que está muy bueno.
We have a wine from the California that is very good.
Rosita es una chica que siempre está dispuesta a ayudar.
Rosita is a girl who is always ready to help.

The forms **el/la/los/las que** are combinations of the definite article and the reflexive pronoun **que**. The article agrees in gender and number with the reference word. Compare the following:
La computadora que tengo en la oficina es mucho mejor.
The computer that I have in the office is much better.
El que tengo en la oficina es mucho mejor.
The one I have in the office is much better.

Prepositions can also be used before **el/la/los/las que:**
¡Por fin vamos a ver las pirámides de las que tanto nos ha hablado Rosita!
At last we are going to see the pyramids, which Rosita has told us so much about!

The expression **lo que** means *what* (*that which*):
¿Sabes lo que pasa?
Do you know what's going on?

§36 Question Words

¿Qué?	*What?*
¿Cómo?	*How?*
¿Dónde?	*Where?*
¿De dónde?	*From where?*
¿Adónde?	*To where?*
¿Quién?	*Who? Whom?*
¿Quiénes?	*Who? Whom?*
¿Cuánto?	*How much?*
¿Cuánto/-a/-os/-as?	*How many?*
¿Por qué?	*Why?*
¿Cuándo?	*When?*
¿A qué hora?	*At what time?*
¿Cuál?	*Which? (singular)*
¿Cuáles?	*Which? (plural)*

Y tú, ¿qué haces? *And what are you doing?*
¿Cómo se llama usted? *What is your name?*
¿Dónde vives? *Where do you live?*
¿De dónde eres? *Where are you from?*
¿Adónde vas? *Where are you going?*
¿Quién es esa persona? *Who is that person?*
¿Quiénes son ustedes? *Who are you (people)?*
¿Cuánto cuesta? *How much does it cost?*
¿Cuántos euros tienes? *How many euros do you have?*
¿Por qué no has ido al cine? *Why didn't you go to the movie?*
¿Cuándo tienes tiempo? *When do you have time?*
¿A qué hora quedamos? *When shall we meet?*
¿Cuál te gusta? *Which one do you like?*
¿Cuáles te gustan? *Which ones do you like?*

§ 37 Prepositions

In the masculine singular, the prepositions **a** and **de** combine with the definite article to form a single word:

a + el ▸ al ¿Vamos **al** museo?
Are we going to the museum?

de + el ▸ del El hotel está enfrente **del** cine.
The hotel is across from the movie theater.

The Preposition *a*

The preposition **a** is used to specify direction and location:

Voy a la biblioteca. – *I am going to the library.*
Vamos al cine. – *We are going to the movie theater.*
¿Vas a casa? – *Are you going home?*
Tiene que girar a la derecha y tomar la primera calle a la izquierda.
You have to turn right and take the first street on the left.

The Preposition *de*

Specifying quantities always involves using the preposition **de**:

un kilo de fresas – *a kilo of strawberries*
medio kilo de tomates – *half a kilo of tomatoes*

The preposition **de** is also used in distinguishing times of the day:

Son las diez de la mañana.
It is ten o'clock in the morning.
Son las diez de la noche.
It is ten o'clock at night.

The Preposition *en*

The preposition en is used with means of transportation:

¿Vas en coche o en autobús?
Are you going by car or bus?

There is one exception: **ir a pie** *(to go by foot)*

The Preposition *para*

The preposition **para** is used to express a purpose:

¿Tiene algo para el dolor?
Do you have anything for pain?

para can also be used with an infinitive (*in order to…*):

Para ir en moto necesitas el casco.
You need a helmet to ride a motorcycle.

The Preposition *por*

The preposition **por** is used with times of the day:

por la mañana   *in the morning*
por la tarde   *in the afternoon*
por la noche   *in the night / evening*

The TemporalPrepositions
desde / hace / desde hace

hace + time *(ago)*

Empezamos hace medio año aproximadamente.
We started about a year ago.

desde + time *(since)*

Mis amigas y yo vamos al bingo desde abril.
My friends and I have been going to bingo since April.

desde hace + time *(for)*

Mis amigas y yo vamos al bingo desde hace medio año.
My friends and I have been going to bingo for six months.

§38 Numbers

0 **cero**	28 **veintiocho**	1000 **mil**
1 **uno**	29 **veintinueve**	1001 **mil uno**
2 **dos**	30 **treinta**	1100 **mil cien**
3 **tres**	31 **treinta y uno**	1999 **mil novecientos noventa**
4 **cuatro**	32 **treinta y dos**	**y nueve**
5 **cinco**	33 **treinta y tres**	2000 **dos mil**
6 **seis**	34 **treinta y cuatro**	3000 **tres mil**
7 **siete**	35 **treinta y cinco**	10.000 **diez mil**
8 **ocho**	40 **cuarenta**	100.000 **cien mil**
9 **nueve**	41 **cuarenta y uno**	1.000.000 **un millón**
10 **diez**	42 **cuarenta y dos**	2.000.000 **dos millones**
11 **once**	43 **cuarenta y tres**	3.000.000 **tres millones**
12 **doce**	50 **cincuenta**	1.000.000.000 **mil millones**
13 **trece**	60 **sesenta**	
14 **catorce**	70 **setenta**	
15 **quince**	80 **ochenta**	
16 **dieciséis**	90 **noventa**	
17 **diecisiete**	100 **cien**	
18 **dieciocho**	101 **ciento uno**	
19 **diecinueve**	110 **ciento diez**	
20 **veinte**	200 **doscientos**	
21 **veintiuno**	300 **trescientos**	
22 **veintidós**	400 **cuatrocientos**	
23 **veintitrés**	500 **quinientos**	
24 **veinticuatro**	600 **seiscientos**	
25 **veinticinco**	700 **setecientos**	
26 **veintiséis**	800 **ochocientos**	
27 **veintisiete**	900 **novecientos**	

A

	a	at, to
	¿a cuántos?	how much?
	¿a dónde?	(to) where?
	a él	to him
	a ella	to her
	a ellos/as	to them
	a fondo	thoroughly
	a la brasa	grilled
	a la derecha (de)	to the right (of)
	a la gallega	in the Gallician manner
	a la izquierda (de)	to the left (of)
	a la romana	breaded
	a mediados	in the middle of
	a menudo	often
	a mí	to me
	a nadie	to nobody
	a nosotros/as	to us
	a partir	starting with
	a pie	on foot
	a ti	to you (sing. inf.)
	a todo el mundo	to everyone
	a todos/as	to all
	a usted	to you (sing. pol.)
	a ustedes	to you (pl. pol.)
	a vosotros/as	to you (pl. inf.)
	abanicar	to fan
el	abogado	lawyer
el	abril	April
	abrir	to open
	abrirse	to open up
la	abuela	grandmother
la	abuelita	grandma
el	abuelito	grandfather
el	abuelo	grandfather
	aburrir	to bore
	aburrirse	to be bored
	acabar	to end, finish
	acabar de	to have just done something
la	academia	academy
la	academia de cine	film academy
el	aceite	oil
el	aceite de oliva	olive oil

	acompañar	to accompany
	acordar	to agree
	acordarse	to remember
	acordarse de	to remember someone or something
	acortar por	to shorten
	acostarse	to go to bed
	acostumbrarse	to get used to
la	actividad	activity
	activo/a	active
el	actor	actor
	adelantar a	to pass someone
	además	in addition
	adiós	good-bye
	afeitarse	to shave
	afortunadamente	fortunately
el	agosto	August
	agradable	agreeable, pleasant
el	agua (f.)	water
	ahora	now
	ahorrar	to save
el	aire	air
el	ajo	garlic
	al	to the
	al ajillo	with garlic sauce
	al cabo	at the end
	al lado (de)	beside
el	albañil	mason
el	alcohol	alcohol
	alcohólico/a	alcoholic
	alegre	happy
	alemán	German (m.)
	alemana	German (f.)
	Alemania	Germany
	alguna vez	sometime
	alguno/a	someone
	allí	over there
la	altura	height
	amable	friendly
	amarillo/a	yellow
	amazónico/a	Amazon
	América	America
la	amiga	friend (f.)
el	amigo	friend (m.)

	añadir	to add
	Andalucía	Andalusia
los	Andes	the Andes
el	anillo	ring
el	animal	animal
el	año	year
	Año Nuevo	New Year
	antes	before
	antiguo/a	old
	aparcar en	park in
el	apellido	last name
	aplaudir	to applaud
	aprender	to learn
	aprender a	lernen zu
	apto para	to learn how to
	aquí	here
	Argentina	Argentina
la	argentina	Argentine (f.)
el	argentino	Argentine (m.)
el	armario	cupboard, closet
el/la	arquitecto/a	architect
el	arte	art
la	artesanía	crafts
el	artículo	article
el/la	artista	artist
	así	thus
	Asturias	Asturias
la	atención	attention
	atraer	to attract
	atravesar	to cross
	atreverse a	to dare
	aunque	although
	Australia	Australia
	Austria	Austria
	austriaco/a	Austrian
el	autobús	bus
la	aventura	adventure
	aventurero/a	adventurous
el	avión	airplane
	ayer	yesterday
	ayudar	to help
el	azúcar	sugar
	azul	blue

B

	bailar	to dance
	bajar	to descend
	bajar a	to go downstairs
el	baloncesto	basketball
	bañar	to bathe, swim
el	baño	bath, bathroom
el	bar	bar
el	barco	ship
el	barrio	neighborhood
	Basilea	Basel
	bastante	rather
	beber	to drink
la	bebida	drink
la	beca	scholarship
	belga	Belgian (m./f.)
	Bélgica	Belgium
	Berlín	Berlin
la	biblioteca	library
la	bicicleta	bicycle
	bien	well
el	billete	ticket
	Blancanieves	Snow White
	blanco/a	white
la	boda	marriage
el	bolígrafo	pen
	Bolivia	Bolivia
	boloñesa	Bolognese
la	bolsa	bag
el	bolso	purse
la	bombilla	lightbulb
los	bombones	bonbons
	bonito/a	pretty
el	bosque	woods
	brillante	brilliant
	Bruselas	Brussels
	buen	good (apocope)
	buenas noches	good evening, good night
	buenas tardes	good afternoon
	buenísimo/a	very good
	bueno/a	good
	buenos días	hello, good day
	buscar	to look for

C

el	caballo	horse
la	cabeza	head
el	cacao	cocoa
el	café	coffee
la	caja	cash register, box
la	calabaza	pumpkin
el	calamar	squid
los	calamares a la romana	breaded squid
	caliente	warm, hot
la	calle	street
el	calor	heat, warmth
la	cama	bed
la	cámara fotográfica	camera
el/la	camarero/a	waiter
	cambiar	to change
el	cambio	change
	caminar	to walk
el	camino	road
el	Camino de Santiago	pilgimage route to Santiago
el	campo	field, countryside
las	Canarias	Canary Islands
la	canción	song
	cansado/a	tired
el	cansancio	fatigue
el/la	cantante	singer
	cantar	to sing
	Caperucita Roja	Little Red Riding Hood
la	caperuza	cap
el	capital	capital
la	capital	capital city
la	cara	face
el	Caribe	Caribbean
la	carne	meat
	caro/a	expensive
la	carpintería	carpentry
la	carretera	highway, road
el	carro	car, wagon
la	carroza	coach
la	carta	letter
la	carta de amor	love letter

el	cartel	sign
el/la	cartero/a	mail carrier
la	casa	house
	casarse	to get married
el	casino	casino
la	casita	little house
el	caso	case
la	catedral	cathedral
la	categoría	category
la	cebolla	onion
la	celebración	celebration dinner
la	cena	dinner
	cenar	to have dinner
el	cenicero	ashtray
	Cenicienta	Cinderella
el	centro	center
	cerca (de)	near
	cero	zero
	cerrar	to close
la	cerveza	beer
la	cesta	basket
la	chaqueta	jacket
la	chaqueta de piel	leather jacket
el/la	chico/a	boy, girl
el	chile	chili
	chileno/a	Chilean
	chino	Chinese
el	chocolate	chocolate
	cien	hundred
	cierto	true, certain
	cinco	five
el	cine	movie
el	circo	circus
	circular por	to circulate through
la	cita	appointment, date
la	ciudad	city
el	ciudadano	resident
	claro	clear
la	clase	class
	clasificar	to classify
el	cliente	client
el	clima	climate
	cocer	to cook
el	coche	car

	cocinar	to cook		cortar	to cut
el/la	cocinero/a	chef, cook		corto/a	short
el	cóctel	cocktail	la	cosa	thing
el	colegio	school	la	costa	coast
	colgar	to hang (up)		costar	to cost
el	color	color	la	costumbre	custom, habit
el	comedor	dining room		creer	to believe
	comentar	to comment		cruzar	to cross
el	comentario	commentary	el	cuaderno	notebook
	comer	to eat	el	cuadro	picture
la	comida	food		¿cuál?	which?
la	comida de lata	canned food		¿cuáles?	which (ones)?
	como	as		cuando	when
	¿cómo?	what?		¿cuándo?	when?
la	compañía	company		¿cuánto?	how much?
la	compañía de discos	record company		¿cuántos?	how many?
	comprar	to buy		cuatro	four
	comprender	to understand		Cuba	Cuba
la	comunicación	communication		cubano/a	Cuban
	comunicado/a	connected		cubrir	to cover
	con	with	el	cuidado	care
	conceder	to concede		cuidar	to be careful, take
el	concierto	concert			care of
el	concierto	open-air concert		culto/a	cultured
	al aire libre		la	cultura	culture
el	concurso	contest		cultural	cultural
	condimentar	to spice	el	cumpleaños	birthday
	conducir	to drive		cumplir	to complete
	conectar	to connect	el	curso	course
	conmigo	with me			
	conocer	to know, meet	**D**		
	conocido	well known			
	conseguir	to obtain		danés	Danish (m.)
el	consejo	advice		danesa	Danish (f.)
	contar	to count		dar	to give
	contigo	with you		dar igual	not to matter
el	contraste	contrast		dar la vuelta	to turn around
la	corbata	necktie		de	from
la	corbata de seda	silk necktie		de dónde	from where?
	Córdoba	Cordoba		de pequeño/a	as a child
el	coro	chorus, choir		de pronto	hastily
	Correos	post office		de repente	suddenly
	correr	to run		debajo (de)	under
	correr peligro	to run a risk	los	deberes	homework
				decidir	to decide

	decir	to say
la	decisión	decision
	decorar	to decorate
	dedicarse	to devote oneself
	dedicarse a	to occupy oneself with
	definir	to define
	dejar	to leave
	dejar de	to stop
	del	from the
	delante (de)	in front (of)
	delgado/a	slender, thin
	demasiado	too much
	demostrar	to demonstrate, show
	depende	it depends
el	deporte	sport
	deprisa	quickly
	derecha	right
el	Derecho	law
el	Derecho Comercial	commercial law
el	desarrollo	development
	descansar	to rest
	descansar en	to rest in
	describir	to describe
	descubrir	to discover
	desde	for (some time)
	desde hace	since
el	despacho	office
	despacio	slowly
la	despedida	good-bye
	despertarse	to wake up
	después	after
	destino a	headed for
	desvestirse	to undress
	desayunar	to have breakfast
el	detalle	detail
	detenidamente	thoroughly
	detrás (de)	behind
el	día	day
el	diente	tooth
el	diente de ajo	clove of garlic
	diez	ten
	diferente	different
la	dificultad	difficulty
	¡dígame!	say! / tell me!
	Dinamarca	Denmark

el	dinero	money
la	dirección	address
el	director	director
el	disco	record
la	discoteca	discotheque
	disculpar	to excuse
el	discurso	discourse
	disponer de	to have available
	diverso/a	diverse
	divertido/a	funny
	divertirse	to have fun
	doce	twelve
la	docena	dozen
el	documental	documentary film
el	documento	document
el	domicilio	residence
el	domingo	Sunday
el	dominó	domino
	donde	where, in which
	dónde	where?
	dormir	to sleep
	dos	two
la	ducha	shower
	ducharse	to take a shower
	durante	during

E

	echar	to throw
	echar de menos	to miss
	echarse a	to do something suddenly
la	economía	economy
	económico/a	economical
el	edificio	building
el	ejercicio	exercise
el	ejercicio de gramática	grammar exercise
	el	the
	él	he
	eléctrico/a	electric
	elegir	to choose, select
	ella	she
	ellos/as	they
	e-mail	e-mail

	empacar	to pack		la	escalada	climb
	empezar	to begin			escalar	to climb
	empezar a	to begin to		el	escalón	stair, step
la	empresa	the company		el	escaparate	display window
la	empresa de mudanza	the moving company			escribir	to write
					escrito/a	written
	en	in, on, at			escuchar	to listen
	en el fondo	basically		la	escuela	school
	en huelga	on strike			ese/a	that one
	en otras palabras	in other words			eso	that
	en primera	first class		los	espaguetis	spaghetti
	en principio	fundamentally			España	Spain
	¿en serio?	really?		el	español	Spaniard (m.)
	en serio	really, seriously			español	Spanish
	en todo caso	in any case		la	española	Spaniard (f.)
	enamorado/a	in love			española	Spanish
el	enanito	dwarf			especial	special
	encantado/a	pleased			especialmente	especially
	encantar	to enchant		el	espectáculo	show
	Encarna	short form of Encarnación		el	espejo	mirror
					esperar	to wait, hope
	encima (de)	on top of, on			esquiar	to ski
	encontrar	to find, meet		la	esquina	corner
	enfadado/a	angry			esta	this (f.)
	enfadar	to get angry		el	estadio	stadium
	enfermar	to become ill			Estados Unidos	United States
la	enfermera	nurse		la	estancia	stay
	enfermo/a	sick		la	estantería	shelf
el/la	enfermo/a	sick person			estar	to be
	enfrente (de)	across (from)			estar de mal humor	to be in a bad mood
	ensayar	to practice, rehearse			estas	these (f. pl.)
	enseguida	immediately			este	this (m.)
	enseñar	to show			estimado/a	dear
	enseñar a	to teach, show			esto	this (neut.)
	entender	to understand		el	estómago	stomach
	entero/a	entire			estos	these (m. pl.)
	entonces	then		el	estrés	stress
la	entrada	entry		el/la	estudiante	student
	entrar en	to enter into			estudiar	to study
	entre	between		el	euro	euro
el	entusiamo	enthusiasm			evitar	to avoid
	envenenado/a	poisoned		el	examen	exam, test
el	equipo	team		la	excursión	excursion
	es un placer	it's a pleasure		la	excusa	excuse

el	éxito	success
	exótico/a	exotic
	explicar	to explain
la	Expo	expo
la	exposición	exposition
el	extranjero	foreigner

F

	fácil	easy
la	facultad	faculty
la	falda	skirt
	faltar	to be lacking
la	fama	fame
la	familia	family
	famoso/a	famous
la	fantasía	fantasy
	fantástico/a	fantastic
la	farmacia	pharmacy
	fascinar	to fascinate
	favorito/a	favorite
el	fax	fax
la	fecha	date
la	fecha de nacimiento	date of birth
la	fiesta	party
la	figura	face
el	fin de semana	weekend
el	finlandés	Finn (m.)
la	finlandesa	Finn (f.)
	Finlandia	Finland
el	flash	flash
la	flauta	flute
el	flautista de Hamelin	Pied Piper of Hameln
la	flor	flower
la	forma	form
la	foto	photo
la	fotografía	photograph
	fotografiar	to photograph
el/la	fotógrafo/a	photographer
	francés	French
el	francés	Frenchman
la	francesa	Frenchwoman

	Francia	France
	freír	to fry
la	fresa	strawberry
	fresco/a	fresh
	frío/a	cold
la	frontera	border
la	fruta	fruit
	fumar	to smoke
la	furgoneta	van
el	fútbol	soccer
el/la	futbolista	soccer player
el	futuro	future

G

	Galicia	Galicia
	ganar	to earn, win
las	ganas	desire
el	gato	cat
el	gazpacho	gazpacho
	genial	nice
la	gente	people
la	gimnasia	gymnastics
el	gimnasio	gym, fitness center
	grabar	to record
	gracias	thanks
	gracias por	thanks for
el	grafiti	graffiti
la	gramática	grammar
	gran	large
	grande	big
la	grasa	fat
	Grecia	Greece
el/la	griego/a	Greek
el	grupo	group
el	grupo de montaña	hiking group
	guapísimo/a	very pretty
	guapo/a	handsome
	guardar	to keep
	guatemalteco/a	Guatemalan
el/la	guía turística	tourist guide
la	guitarra	guitar
	gustar	to be pleasing
el	gusto	taste

H

	haber	to have
el/la	habitante	inhabitant
	hablar	to speak
	hace	ago
	hacer	to make, do
	hacia	toward
el	hambre	hunger
	Hamburgo	Hamburg
	hasta	until
	hasta luego	see you later
	hasta pronto	see you soon
	hay	there is, there are
	helado/a	frozen
la	hermanita	little sister
el	hermanito	little brother
el/la	hermano/a	brother, sister
los	hermanos	brothers and sisters
el/la	hijo/a	son, daughter
la	Historia	history
	histórico/a	historic
	hola	hi
	Holanda	Holland
el	holandés	Dutch (m.)
la	holandesa	Dutch (f.)
el	hombre	man
la	hora	hour, time
la	hora de trabajo	work hour
el	hospital	hospital
el	hotel	hotel
	hoy	today
el	huevo	egg
el	humor	humor

I

la	idea	idea
el	idioma	language
la	iglesia	church
	igual	same
la	imaginación	imagination
el	imperativo	imperative
el	imperfecto	imperfect

	importante	important
	importar	to be important, to matter
la	impresora	printer
el	impuesto	tax
la	inauguración	opening
	incluir	to include
el	indefinido	indefinite past
las	Indias	Indies
	indígena	indigenous
el/la	indígena	native
la	infancia	infancy, childhood
la	influencia	influence
	informarse de	to find out about
la	Informática	computer science
la	infusión	herbal tea
	Inglaterra	England
	inglés	English
el	inglés	Englishman
la	inglesa	Englishwoman
el	ingrediente	ingredient
	inteligente	intelligent
	intensamente	intensely
	intentar	to try
	interesante	interesting
	interesar	to interest
el	interior del país	interior
	internacional	international
el	internet	Internet
	inventar	to invent
	investigar	to investigate
el	invierno	winter
el	invitado	guest
	invitar	to invite
	ir	to go
	ir a	to go to
el/la	iraquí	Iraqi
	irse	to leave, go
la	isla	the island
las	Islas Canarias	Canary Islands
las	Islas Galápagos	Galapagos Islands
el/la	israelí	Israeli
	Italia	Italy
el/la	italiano/a	Italian

J

el	jabón	soap
el	jardín	garden, yard
el	jazz	jazz
el	jefe	boss, chief
	joven	young
el	juego	game
	jugar	to play
	jugar a las cartas	to play cards
	jugar al fútbol	to play soccer
	jugar al golf	to play golf
	jugar al tenis	to play tennis
el	juguete	toy
el	julio	July
	junto/a	with

K

el	kilómetro	kilometer

L

	la	the (f. sing.), her
el	lado	side
la	lámpara	lamp
	las	the (f. pl.), them
el/la	latino/a	Latin American
	Latinoamérica	Latin America
el	lavabo	sink, bathroom
la	lavadora	washing machine
	lavarse	to wash (oneself)
el	lazo	lasso
	le	to/for him, her, you (formal)
la	leche	milk
	leer	to read
	lejos (de)	far (from)
la	lengua	language, tongue
	lentamente	slowly
	les	to/for you, them
	levantarse	to get up
la	libertad	liberty, freedom

la	libra	pound (English)
	libre	free
la	librería	bookstore
el	libro	book
	limitar	to limit
	limitarse a	to limit oneself to
la	limonada	lemonade, soft drink
la	línea	line
el	líquido	liquid
	Lisboa	Lisbon
el	litro	liter
	llamar	to call, phone
	llamarse	to be called
la	llave	key
	llegada a	arrival
	llegar	to arrive
	llegar a	to arrive at
	lleno/a	full
	llevar	to carry, bring
	llover	to rain
	lo	it, him
	lo mejor	the best
el	lobo	wolf
	localizar	to locate
	los	the (m. pl.), them
	luchar	to struggle, fight
	luchar por	to fight for
	luego	later, then
el	lugar	place
el	lugar de nacimiento	place of birth
el	lunes	Monday
	Luxemburgo	Luxemburg
el	luxemburgués	Luxemburger (m.)
la	luxemburguesa	Luxemburger (f.)

M

la	madre	mother
	mal	badly
	malo/a	bad
la	mamá	mom
	mañana	tomorrow
la	mañana	morning

la	mano	hand		el	miércoles	Wednesday
	mantenerse	to support oneself		la	miga	crumb
la	manzana	apple		la	miga de pan	breadcrumb
	maquillarse	to put on makeup			mío/a	mine
la	maquinilla	razor			¡mira!	look!
la	maquinilla	electric razor			mirar	to look
	eléctrica				mis	my
el	mar	ocean, sea		la	mochila	backpack
la	marcha	march			moderno/a	modern
	marchar	to march			molestar	to bother
	marcharse	to leave		el	momento	moment
el	marco	frame		la	montaña	mountain
el	marco de plata	silver frame		el	monumento	monument
el	martes	Tuesday			morir	to die
	más	more			morir de	to die of
	más (…) que	more … than			morirse de ganas	to be dying to
las	Matemáticas	mathematics		el	mosquito	mosquito
	matricularse	to enroll		la	motocicleta	motorcycle
el	mayo	May			mover	to move
	mayor	older, larger		el	móvil	cell phone
la	mayoría	majority			muchas gracias	thanks a lot
	me	me			muchas veces	often
	me llamo	my name is			muchísimo/a	very much
la	médica	(female) doctor			mucho	much
la	medicina	medicine			mucho gusto	pleased to meet you
el	medio	medium			mucho/a	move
el	medio de	means of		la	mudanza	woman
	comunicación	communication		el	mundo	world
	medio/a	half		la	muñeca	doll
	mejor	better		la	muñeca de trapo	rag doll
	mejorar	to improve			Múnich	Munich
	menos	less		el	museo	museum
el	menú del día	the daily special		la	música	music
el	mercado	market			muy	very
el	mes	month				
la	mesa	table		**N**		
el	metal	metal				
el	metro	metro		el	nacimiento	birth
el/la	mexicano/a	Mexican			nada	nothing
	México	Mexico			nadar	to swim
	mezclar	to mix			nadie	no one, nobody
	mi	my		la	naranja	orange
el	miedo	fear		la	naturaleza	nature
	mientras	during				

la	Navidad	*Christmas*
	necesitar	*to need*
	negar	*to deny*
	negarse a	*to refuse to*
	nervioso/a	*nervous*
	nevar	*to snow*
	ningún	*no one*
	ninguno/a	*none*
el/la	niño/a	*boy, girl*
	no	*no, not*
la	noche	*night*
el	nombre	*name*
	normalmente	*normally*
el	norte	*north*
	Noruega	*Norway*
el/la	noruego/a	*Norwegian*
	nos	*us*
	nosotros/as	*we*
la	nota	*note*
la	noticia	*notice, news*
las	noticias deportivas	*sporting news*
la	novela	*novel*
la	novia	*girlfriend, fiancée*
el	novio	*boyfriend, fiancé*
	nublado	*cloudy*
	nuestro/a	*our*
	nueve	*nine*
	nuevo/a	*new*
el	número	*number*
	nunca	*never*

O

	o	*or*
la	obligación	*obligation*
	obligar	*to force*
la	obra de teatro	*play*
	observar	*to observe*
la	ocasión	*occasion, opportunity*
el	océano	*ocean*
el	Océano Pacífico	*Pacific Ocean*
	ocho	*eight*
la	oficina	*office*
	ofrecer	*to offer*

	oír	*to hear*
el	ojo	*eye*
	olvidar	*to forget*
	olvidarse de	*to forget something*
la	ópera	*opera*
	opinar	*to feel, be of the opinion*
el	ordenador (Spain)	*computer*
	ordenar	*to straighten up*
la	orquesta	*orchestra*
	os	*you (fam. pl., direct / ind. obj.)*
el	oso	*bear*
el	otoño	*fall, autumn*
	otra vez	*again*
	otro/a	*another*
	¡oye!	*listen!*

P

el	paciente	*patient*
el	Pacífico	*pacific*
el	padre	*father*
los	padres	*parents*
la	paella	*paella*
	pagar	*to pay*
el	país	*country*
el	paisaje	*landscape*
el	pájaro	*bird*
la	palabra	*word*
el	pan	*bread*
la	panadería	*bakery*
la	Panamericana	*Pan-American Highway*
el	pantalón	*pants*
el	papel	*paper*
el	paquete	*package*
	para	*for, (in order) to*
	parecer	*to appear*
	parecerse	*to resemble*
la	pared	*wall*
	París	*Paris*
el	parque	*park*
	¡pasa!	*come in!*
el	pasado	*past*

el/la	pasajero/a	*passenger*
	pasar	*to pass*
	pasar miedo	*to be afraid (of)*
	pasar por	*to go through*
	pasear	*to stroll*
la	pasta	*pasta*
la	patata	*potato*
las	patatas fritas	*french fries*
las	papas bravas	*potatoes with a spicy sauce*
el	patito	*duckling*
el	pato	*duck*
	pedir	*to order*
	peinarse	*to comb one's hair*
	pelar	*to peel*
la	película	*film*
la	película de terror	*horror movie*
el	peligro	*danger*
	peligroso/a	*dangerous*
la	pelota	*ball*
la	peluquería	*hair salon*
	pensar	*to think*
	pensar en	*to think about*
el	pepino	*cucumber*
	pequeño/a	*small, little*
	perder	*to lose*
el	periódico	*newspaper*
el	periodista	*journalist*
el	periodo	*period*
	permitir	*to allow, permit*
	pero	*but*
el	perro	*dog*
la	persona	*person*
	personal	*personal*
la	perspectiva	*perspective*
	pertenecer	*to belong*
	Perú	*Peru*
el/la	pianista	*pianist*
	picante	*spicy*
el	pie	*foot*
la	piel	*skin*
	pintar	*to paint*
la	piscina	*swimming pool*
el	piso	*apartment*

la	pizza	*pizza*
el	placer	*pleasure*
	planear	*to plan*
la	plata	*silver*
el	plátano	*banana*
el	plato	*plate*
la	playa	*beach*
la	plaza	*square*
el	plural	*plural*
	poco	*little*
	poder	*to be able*
el	poder	*power*
la	policía	*police*
la	política	*politics*
	político/a	*political*
el	pollo	*chicken*
el	pollo al ajillo	*chicken in garlic sauce*
	poner	*to put, place*
	poner en marcha	*to start*
	poner la mesa	*to set the table*
	poquito/a	*little*
	por	*for*
	por cierto	*by the way, incidentally*
	por completo	*completely*
	por el camino	*on the road, en route*
	por eso	*therefore*
	por favor	*please*
	por fin	*finally*
	¿por qué?	*why?*
	por supuesto	*of course*
	porque	*because*
el	porqué	*reason*
el	portugués	*Portuguese (m.)*
la	portuguesa	*Portuguese (f.)*
la	posición	*position*
la	postal	*postcard*
	practicar	*to practice, rehearse*
	precioso/a	*charming*
	preferido/a	*favorite*
	preferir	*to prefer*
	preguntar	*to ask*
la	prensa	*press*
	preocupar	*to worry*
	preparar	*to prepare*

	presentar	to present/display
	prestar	to loan
	prestar atención	to pay attention
	primero/a	first
el/la	primo/a	cousin
	principal	main
el	príncipe	prince
la	prisa	rush
	privado/a	private
el	problema	problem
la	profesión	profession
el	profesor	teacher (m.)
la	profesora	teacher (f.)
	prohibido/a	forbidden
	pronto	soon
	proponerse	to propose
	próximo/a	next
el	público	public
el	pueblo	people, town
la	puerta	door
	pues	so
el	puesto de trabajo	workplace
el	pulpo	octopus
el	pulpo a la gallega	octopus cooked in the Galician manner
	pulsar	to press, push
	puntual	punctual

Q

	¿qué?	what?
	que	that, which
	¡qué se mejore!	get better!
	¡qué sorpresa!	what a surprise!
	¿qué tal?	how goes it?
	quedar	to remain
	quejar	to complain
	querer	to like, love
	querido/a	dear
	¿quién?	who? (sing.)
	¿quiénes?	who? (pl.)
	quince	fifteen
	quitar	to leave, remove

R

la	radio	radio
	rápidamente	quickly
	rápido/a	quick
	raro/a	rare
la	razón	reason
la	realidad	reality
la	receta	recipe
	recomendar	recommend
	recto	straight ahead
el	recuerdo	memory
la	redacción	writing, editorial office
	redactar	to write
	referirse a	to refer tof
	reforzar	to reinforce, strengthen
el	refresco	soft drink
	regalar	to give (a gift)
la	región	region
	reír	to laugh
el	repelente	insect repellent
	repetir	to repeat
el	resfriado	cold
	resfriado/a	sick with a cold
el	respeto	respect
el	responsable	person in charge
	responsable	responsible
el	restaurante	restaurant
la	reunión	reunion
	reunir	to bring together
la	revista	magazine
la	revista de moda	fashion magazine
el	rezante	person praying
el	río	river
	riquísimo/a	very delicious
	robar	to steal
	rodar	to film
	rojo/a	red
	Roma	Rome
la	ropa	clothing
la	rosa	rose
el	ruido	noise

S

	saber	to know
la	sal	salt
	salida de	exit, departure from
	salir	to depart, leave
	salir a	to go out
el	salón	living room
la	salsa	sauce
la	salsa boloñesa	Bolognese sauce
el	saludo	greeting
	sano/a	healthy
la	sauna	sauna
	se	oneself, him/herself, themselves, yourself, yourselves
	se llama	is called, is named
la	secretaria	secretary
el	secreto	secret
la	seda	silk
	seguir	to follow, continue
	segundo/a	second
	seguramente	surely
	seguro	sure
	seguro/a	certain
	seis	six
la	selva	forest
la	Selva Negra	Black Forest
la	semana	week
la	Semana Santa	Holy Week
el	señor	man
el	Señor de los Anillos	The Lord of the Rings
la	señora	lady
	sentarse	to sit down
	sentir	to feel
el	septiembre	September
	ser	to be
	ser cuestión de	to be a question of
	serio/a	serious
	servir	to serve
	sí	yes
	si	if, whether
	siempre	always
la	siesta	siesta
	siete	seven
la	silla	chair
	simpático/a	nice
	sin	without
	sincero/a	sincere
el	singular	singular
el	sistema inmune	immune system
el	sitio	place, location
la	situación	situation
la	situación económica	economic situation
	situado/a	located
	sobre	on, concerning
	sobre todo	especially
el	sol	sun
	soler	to be in the habit of doing something
	sólo	only
	solo/a	alone
la	solución	solution
	soñar	to dream
la	sopa	soup
la	sopa de sobre	soup from a packet
la	sorpresa	surprise
	su	his, her, its, their, your
la	subida	rise
	subir a	to go up
el	subte	metro, subway
	Sudamérica	South America
	Suecia	Sweden
el/la	sueco/a	Swede
el	sueño	dream
la	suerte	luck
el	supermercado	supermarket
el	sur	south

T

	también	also
	tampoco	neither
	tan	so
el	tango	tango
	tanto/a	so much
la	tarde	afternoon

la	tarta	*pie*
la	tarta de fresa	*strawberry pie*
el	taxi	*taxi*
	te	*to / for you, you (dir. obj.)*
el	té	*tea*
el	teatro	*theater*
la	tecla	*key (keyboard)*
la	tele	*television*
el	teléfono	*telephone*
el	teléfono móvil	*cell phone*
la	televisión	*television*
	televisivo/a	*television (adj.)*
el	tema	*subject*
	tener	*to have*
	tener cuidado	*to be careful*
	tener hambre	*to be hungry*
	tener razón	*to be right*
el	tenis	*tennis*
	tercero/a	*third*
	terminar	*to end*
	terrible	*terrible*
el	terror	*terror*
el	testigo	*witness*
el	tiempo	*weather, time*
el	tiempo libre	*free time*
la	tienda de campaña	*tent*
	tímido/a	*timid*
el	tipo	*type*
el	título	*title*
	tocar	*to play*
	todavía	*still*
	todavía no	*not yet*
	todo	*everything*
	todo/a	*all*
	todos los días	*every day*
	tomar	*to take, drink*
el	tomate	*tomato*
la	tortilla	*omelet*
la	tortilla de papas	*potato omelet*
la	tostada	*toast*

	trabajar	*to work*
el	trabajo	*work*
	traducir	*to translate*
	traer	*to bring*
el	tráfico	*traffic*
el	traje	*suit*
	tranquilamente	*calmly*
la	tranquilidad	*calm (n.)*
	tranquilo/a	*calm (adj.)*
	transmitir	*to transmit*
el	trapo	*rag*
	trasladar	*to move*
el	traslado	*move*
	tratar	*to treat*
	tratar de	*to try*
el	tren	*train*
	tres	*three*
	triste	*sad*
	triturar	*to grind*
el	trozo	*piece*
	tú	*you*
el	túnel	*tunnel*
el	turismo	*tourism*
el	turismo de masas	*mass tourism*
el	turrón	*torrone*

U

	últimamente	*recently*
	último/a	*last*
	un	*one (m. apocope)*
	un día	*one day*
	una	*one (f.)*
el	uniforme	*uniform*
la	universidad	*university*
	uno	*one (m.)*
	unos/as	*some, a few*
	usted	*you (formal)*
	ustedes	*you (pl.)*
	útil para	*useful for*
	utilizar	*to use*

V

las	vacaciones	vacation
	vale	OK
	valiente	brave
el	valor	value
el	vaso	glass
el	vatio	watt
el/la	vecino/a	neighbor
	veinte	twenty
el	vendedor	salesman
	vender	to sell
	venir	to come
	venir a	to come to
la	ventana	window
	ver	to see
	ver a	to see someone
el	verano	summer
el	verbo	verb
	¿verdad?	really? isn't that so? right?
la	verdad	truth
	verdad	true
	verde	green
la	verdulería	fruit and vegetable store
la	verdura	vegetables
	vestirse	to get dressed
la	vez	time
	viajar	to travel
	viajar en	to travel in
el	viaje	trip
la	vida	life
la	vida privada	private life
el	viernes	Friday
el	vinagre	vinegar
el	vino	wine
el	vino tinto	red wine
la	visita	visit
	visitar	to visit
la	vitamina	vitamin
la	vivencia	experience
	vivir	to live
	volar	to fly
el	volcán	volcano
	volver	to return
	vosotros/as	you (pl., fam., Spain)
	vuestro/a	your (pl., fam., Spain)

Y

y	and
ya	already
yo	I

Z

el	zapato	shoe
la	zona verde	green area
el	zoológico	zoo
el	zumo	juice
el	zumo de naranja	orange juice

Photo Credits:

p. 20 *book*—EKS, Inc., Stuttgart
p. 20 *chair*—EKS, Inc., Stuttgart
p. 20 *table*—EKS, Inc., Stuttgart
p. 20, 26 *telephone*—MEV Publishing, Inc.,
      Augsburg
p. 20 *computer*—EKS, Inc., Stuttgart
p. 20 *fax*—EKS, Inc., Stuttgart
p. 20 *lamp*—EKS, Inc., Stuttgart
p. 20, 26 *cell phone*—EKS, Inc., Stuttgart
p. 20 *notebook*—EKS, Inc., Stuttgart
p. 24 *couple of houses* —EKS, Inc., Stuttgart
p. 24 *car*—Nora Deike, Barcelona
p. 24 *couple of lamps* —EKS, Inc., Stuttgart
p. 24 *several books*—EKS, Inc., Stuttgart
p. 24 *couple of computers*—EKS, Inc., Stuttgart
p. 24 *couple of telephones*—EKS, Inc., Stuttgart
p. 24 *several tables*—EKS, Inc., Stuttgart
p. 24 *hospital*—Nora Deike, Barcelona
p. 28 *modern houses*—Nora Deike, Barcelona
p. 28 *a yellow book*—EKS, Inc., Stuttgart
p. 28 *pretty girl*—Nora Deike, Barcelona
p. 28 *fast cars*—Nora Deike, Barcelona
p. 28 *red roses*—EKS, Inc., Stuttgart
p. 30 *Barcelona*—EKS, Inc., Stuttgart
p. 30 *old quarter of Barcelona*—EKS, Inc.,
      Stuttgart
p. 102 *1 kg of potatoes + 6 eggs*—EKS, Inc.,
      Stuttgart
p. 102 *potato peels*—EKS, Inc., Stuttgart
p. 102 *potatoes in a pan*—EKS, Inc., Stuttgart
p. 102 *beating eggs*—EKS, Inc., Stuttgart
p. 102 *flipping a tortilla*—EKS, Inc., Stuttgart

Recording, Editing, and Mastering:
Ton in Ton Medienhaus, Stuttgart

Editing:
ARTist Tonstudios, Pfullingen

Voices:
Monica Cociña Iglesias
Alfred Eichenmüller
Estefanía Férez Bernal
Miguel Freire Gómez
María Engracia López Sánchez
Carlos Ortega Cañado
Alicia Padrós
Ernesto Palaoro
Sabine Sánchez López
Antje Wollenweber

Track List

1

Track　1 – Exercise 1
Track　2 – Exercise 2
Track　3 – Exercise 3
Track　4 – Exercise 4
Track　5 – Exercise 13
Track　6 – Exercise 14
Track　7 – Exercise 16

2

Track　8 – Exercise 2
Track　9 – Exercise 3
Track 10 – Exercise 8
Track 11 – Exercise 11

3

Track 12 – Exercise 1
Track 13 – Exercise 3
Track 14 – Exercise 4
Track 15 – Exercise 8
Track 16 – Exercise 9

4

Track 17 – Exercise 1
Track 18 – Exercise 4
Track 19 – Exercise 7
Track 20 – Exercise 8
Track 21 – Exercise 11

5

Track 22 – Exercise 1
Track 23 – Exercise 2
Track 24 – Exercise 7
Track 25 – Exercise 10
Track 26 – Exercise 15

Test 5

Track 27 – Exercise 1

6

Track 28 – Exercise 1
Track 29 – Exercise 3

Test 6

Track 30 – Exercise 2

7

Track 31 – Exercise 1
Track 32 – Exercise 4
Track 33 – Exercise 14

8

Track 34 – Exercise 1
Track 35 – Exercise 2
Track 36 – Exercise 4
Track 37 – Exercise 5

Test 8

Track 38 – Exercise 3

9

Track 39 – Exercise 1
Track 40 – Exercise 2
Track 41 – Exercise 3
Track 42 – Exercise 5
Track 43 – Exercise 12

10

Track 44 – Exercise 1
Track 45 – Exercise 2
Track 46 – Exercise 3
Track 47 – Exercise 7

Test 10

Track 48 – Exercise 3

11

Track 49 – Exercise 1
Track 50 – Exercise 3
Track 51 – Exercise 4

12

Track 52 – Exercise 1
Track 53 – Exercise 2
Track 54 – Exercise 4
Track 55 – Exercise 9
Track 56 – Exercise 12